JC & Me

To Cathy

Be love.

Design and in-house editing by Joe Blades.
Printed and bound in Canada by Sentinel Printing, Yarmouth NS.

This book is also published by ℗eBooks, ISBN 1-896647-17-0, in a digital PDF binding (for use on any computer with Acrobat Reader 4). Distribution is through the PublishingOnline.Com website.

MARITIMES ARTS PROJECTS PRODUCTIONS
Box 596 Stn A   **www.brokenjaw.com**
Fredericton NB E3B 5A6   tel / fax 506 454-5127
Canada   jblades@nbnet.nb.ca

Canadian Cataloguing in Publication Data
Mouradian, Ted, 1948-

    JC and me

    (YOUR MAPP ; 2)

    ISBN 1-896647-35-9

1. Jesus Christ — Teachings. 2. Love — Biblical teaching. I . Title.
II. Series: YOUR M.A.P.P (Fredericton, N.B.) ; 2

BS2417.L7M68 2000   241'.4   C00-950092-8

JC & Me

TED MOURADIAN

2

Maritimes Arts Projects Productions
Fredericton • Canada

DEDICATION

This vision is dedicated to all people worldwide who are looking to believe in unconditional nonjudgmental love. It is for all of those people who have been disenfranchised because they were perceived as different.

THANKS

I would like to thank all those who looked over the initial manuscript, your feedback was appreciated and insightful.

A special thanks to Leiki Veskimets for her long hours of dedication and for helping me edit my thoughts so that I may bring all of you a clearer vision.

FOREWORD

J.C.'s time on this planet was about love; unconditional nonjudgmental love. This interpretation of what it might, could or would be like if he were here today is my interpretation and only my interpretation.

JC & Me is meant as a wake-up call to all those individuals who would use their positions of power and knowledge to force their beliefs on others. It is not meant to be a trash of any religion, nation or group of people.

It is my hope that *J C & Me* will show you how to love unconditionally. How not to judge or condemn others simply because they do not believe the same things you do. How embrace change and not to fear difference.

Remember, we were all created as individuals. We are all different and different is not bad. I believe that the greatest sin of all is not allowing people to be who they were created to be.

J.C. is about celebrating difference.

J.C. is about unconditional nonjudgmental love.

J. C. is about doing unto others as you would have them do unto you.

"You will be free to be the person you were meant to be

once you allow all others the freedom to be

the people they were meant to be."

— Ted Mouradian

JC & Me

Me: Oh, no! It's 3 in the morning. Boy, is it hot! I can't sleep. Why can't I sleep? This has been one of the hottest summers I've ever experienced. Why can't I sleep? OK, focus. Look around the room and focus on something, anything. Let's see, start on the left and make your way around.

My eyes begin to wander and I try to focus on things that make this space mine. The room is partially lit by the soft glow of the moon, which gives a kind of surreal look to the space.

The first thing I notice is the bookshelf. There aren't a lot of books on the shelf because this is actually where I keep my memorabilia. I notice my golf and bowling trophies. Wow, those were the days, I had so much fun playing those sports. I still do a lot of golfing, but I haven't bowled in a league in years. And there's my treasure. The gold medal that I won for rowing at the Henely. Ah ... memories!

Then there's the window that looks out to the backyard and the trees that have grown to be so magnificent. They seem to protect the house from the elements. I can smell the outside and even though it's the middle of the night, there's this incredible peacefulness.

Next to the window I can see my desk with the computer and all the papers strewn about. My research, the books about religions of the world coupled with the historic aspects of those religions make for quite a pile. Religions and mythology have always fascinated me; why do people believe the things they do? Why have so many religions been used to dominate, control and segregate? Questions, questions, questions ...

Me: OK. Concentrate. Just what exactly are you thinking about? What's on your mind?

Come to think of it ... a hell of a lot! Why do people fight and discriminate? Why are the Arabs fighting the Jews? What's all this stuff about ethnic cleansing? Why are these things allowed to continue? It hurts me to see innocent people being tortured and killed in the name of government or the church.

For example, I read in the paper today about a black football player and his wife putting ads in the paper speaking out against homosexuality. Did he forget so easily how it was illegal to be a free black only decades back? Didn't he remember what could have happened to him if he wanted to marry a white woman? And to think as a part time Baptist minister, he's using Christ's name to discriminate, by using the same ideology that was used against him.

There it is again, religion and in particular, Christianity. Religions should be a good thing. They all talk of a loving, caring God. They speak of a high moral code, of honour, pride, and justice, yet my mind is totally clogged with images of injustice. People killing people in the name of God, religions fighting religions and Nations against Nations. On TV, I've seen the Evangelist shouting fire and brimstone; evoking God's wrath on those who would not agree with his or her narrow view of the Essence of the Bible and God's true intent. How can this God let these atrocities take place, especially in His name? How can Jesus allow people to act the way they do? When I think of the destruction some Christians have caused in the name of love, frankly, it sickens me.

As I think of Jesus, I picture a man who would rather educate than excommunicate. A nonjudgmental, nonviolent, pure-love being.

Me: I really, really wish I had an opportunity to meet and talk to Jesus. It would truly be wonderful to find out what he was thinking during his brief time on this planet and what he thinks of the world today.

As I lay on my back, arms folded behind my head, I stare at the ceiling fan slowly turning. You'd think that the slight hum of the electric motor would lull me to sleep, but it actually seems to keep my mind swirling as if in a hypnotic state. I begin to think what it might be like to actually have a conversation with Christ. Will he be as I envision him? Will he be able to answer the questions that are riddling my mind? Will I have the courage to ask the questions that need to be asked? And, can I handle the answers? Still, it would be a most interesting encounter.

While tossing and turning, I feel a presence slowly fill the room.

Me: Who's there?

JC: You wanted to talk to me?

It seems as if the voice is below me, beside me, above me, behind me and inside me. The voice has a calmness that is almost unsettling. The tone is mellow, yet has strength and conviction that makes you take notice.

The energy in the room is magnetic and a soft glow emanates from inside my closet. I'm curious, yet, not afraid. For some unknown reason I actually feel quite safe.

Me: You say I want to talk to you. Well, who the hell are you? It's 3 am. Is this some sort of a joke?

JC: No. It is no joke. I am Jesus Christ.

Me: What! ... Ya right!

JC: You said you wanted to find out about me. Frankly, I know that you have had a curiosity about me for many years now. And I know that you think of me to be much different than what has been written about me. Well, I am here and I am prepared to tell you all you want to know. So, are you going to invite me in, I am tired of being in this closet.

OK. Calm down. Think about this. There is a voice coming from my closet and this voice says it is Jesus Christ and wants to talk to me. This is weird!

Me: Quit fooling around. Are you really Jesus Christ?

JC: Yes, it is I and I am here as you requested. Hopefully, I will be able to shed some light on some of the misgivings you are having about religion and me in general. You need only to believe. Again, I ask you, may I please come out of the closet?

Me: Oh, Yes ... . I'm sorry. Please come out ... I mean come in.

The light begins to penetrate the door, then fill the room. I try to make out the figure that is standing before me, but it's difficult because of the radiant glow.

Me: Could you please tone down the light a bit? It's hard for me to see what you look like.

JC: I apologize. You see, I keep forgetting My Essence can be a little much. There, is that better?

Me: Yes, much better.

I can't believe it. I simply cannot believe it. Is this really happening, or is it just a dream? What do I do? What do I say? Yet here he stands just to the left of the foot of my bed, his robe is flowing and sort of cream in colour. It's simple, yet elegant. His hair is long and curly. His face sports a neatly trimmed beard and moustache. The olive complexion of his skin only enhances his Mediterranean ancestry. He seems to encompass all of the images of Christ that I've seen over the years.

Me: I thought you'd be taller

Ouch! What a stupid thing to say.

JC: I thought you'd be gayer.

Well ... he has a sense of humour ... this is good.

Me: Touché!

JC: Because I am pure energy and really do not have form, the only form I can be is what you perceive me to be. Therefore, I could be tall, short, young, old, male, female, Asian or a person of colour. What you need is what I become. You are getting my image from what you know. Each person who perceives me is able to conceptualize me in his or her own way.

Me: So, I could make you taller.

JC: Sure if you have to.

Me: No, just kidding. I'm having a hard time believing that you are actually here. How much time do we have together?

JC: As long as you need.

Me: Good, because I want to be able to discuss some very deep concerns I have about your representations, your religion and what you actually were trying to do a few thousand years ago.

JC: First of all, let us correct a misconception. It is not my religion. My name was and is used by others. They were the ones who started Christianity, not me. Among those who started this new religion were my apostles who included Matthew, Mark, Peter and John. Remember, the New Testament Gospels were written decades after my death, then interpreted and reinterpreted.

People were looking for something new to believe in. They needed hope. You have to remember that life was much different back then. Everyone was struggling for survival, tribe against tribe, God against God. There was a definite hierarchy in society, and the peasantry which I was a part of, lived from hand to mouth.

Me: Not much has changed has it?

JC: Sadly, it has not.

I can't stop staring at him. His energy is so pure, so clean.

JC: We keep repeating the same mistakes over and over again. But, truly life was different. People of the time did not have the knowledge or technologies that you have today. We lived a simple life. Villages were small and isolated from each other. There were many different myths, ideologies, traditions and cultural mores. Many people were afraid of the unknown. The few with the knowledge, the temple elders and the ones in power, the Romans, used that power and knowledge to form their views of society at that time.

Survival was dependent on unity and single-minded thinking. In many instances blind faith was the only way to go if a person was to fit in. Think about this. Let us say a person with a charismatic personality said to you that if you committed a certain act, you would be taken from this consciousness and would be burned and tortured in purgatory for eternity. And, if there was no way to counter that argument, such as science, TV or books, generally speaking, you would believe and you would conform and obey. Today there are many ways of proving them wrong. Back then that was not an option. It was an impossibility.

Me: Well, uh …

He raises his left hand slightly and moves a few steps closer.

JC: Do not be frightened. I sense you are hesitating. Ask me anything.

Me: OK. Wasn't a certain amount of that needed to maintain order and frighten your enemy?

JC: True, but many went beyond logic and used mysticism to control. Just look at the moral codes in the Old Testament, many of which cannot be followed and are in fact not followed today.

Me: I only know what I read and what I've been taught. At the time there seemed to have been many Gods all claiming to be "The God."

JC: No, what you had were many men, and yes I say men, for it was the men of the time who had the control. These were the ones who said that *their* God was the only God, that *their* God's law was the only law. Let us look at my ancestors and their struggle for survival and identity.

Me: Before you go on, may I compare the nuclear weapons of today with some of the Gods of the past? In other words, if I had a more powerful God than your God, similar to the nuclear weapons of today, I would hope this would make you think twice before you tried to conquer me and vice versa.

JC: That is a good analogy but I think the power of the God was more to control the people within the village or nation.

Me: You mean more like Santa Claus. If you're not good, according to my rules, you're not going to get the gifts He has for you.

JC: Ah yes, Santa Claus. He is the mythical gift giver that was developed and is associated with the celebration of my birth ...

I can't believe he knows about Santa Claus. If this is my vision, does he know everything I know? It's going to be interesting to see if there is anything that he doesn't know about the world of today.

JC: … And, yes. It is all about coming up with certain rules that must be obeyed. And, if you did not obey the rules, there had to be a punishment strong enough to deter you from breaking the rules.

Me: I see. Now, what about your people?

JC: Let us look at the history, and remember, history is only what we know from what someone told us about the past. If we were not there, we rely on the honesty of the person sharing the history. That is another thing, all events are subject to the perception and interpretation of the person who witnessed the events, as well as the motives behind the way the event was recorded and reported. Therefore, keep this in mind as we continue our interaction. The events and comments that I make about the past are my perceptions of history and further, because this is your dream, it is really your projection of what you believe I would be saying.

Me: Wow! that's deep. And frankly a pretty interesting concept.

JC: So, to continue, the Israelites were a small group of people surrounded by various other groups of people, all trying to survive, each with their special group of Gods. From what we know, it was the Israelites that created the one God theory for the area and the temple elders of the time were able to parley the concept into a major religion, being Judaism, and subsequently, a strong and formidable Nation, the Nation of Israel.

What did he just say? I can't believe I'm hearing this!

Me: Stop right there! It sounds like you're telling me that God was created by man, not that God created man. Are you not the Son of God? Did God not create heaven and earth?

JC: Remember when I said to you that your vision of me is exactly how you see me?

Me: Yes.

JC: Well, God is what man has created. God is neither male nor female. God is pure energy. God is the soul. God is the spark of life that exists in every living thing. Am I the Son of God? I believe I am, for if God is life, then I am part of God for I am life. Was there a God prior to man? Yes and no.

Me: I'm getting confused.

JC: Let me try to explain it this way. I am here in the image that you created. The question is, am I a figment of your imagination or, am I real and therefore, answering your call to me? When you tell people about this conversation, are you going to be hailed as a visionary who actually spoke to and now has a direct pipeline to Christ? Or, are people of the 21st century going to say you made this all up in your mind?

Me: The truth is, there are people who'd say that I made this up because, first, I don't belong to a specific church and secondly, I'm gay, so they would probably wonder how I could have a relationship with you. These same people believe that because I'm gay, religion doesn't factor into my life and they're wrong. I *can* be gay and have a relationship with you. If I remember correctly, you related to the poor, the average, the weak, the disenfranchised, not the elders and lawgivers of the time. So this dream or vision that I'm having could easily be coming from God and I could truly be talking to and getting the true facts from Jesus himself.

JC: Am I not here and do you not believe you are in fact hearing my words?

Me: Yes.

JC: Then for you I am real.

A chill runs up my spine, for I know that he in fact is here and my life will never be the same.

Me: Please … please go on.

He takes a few steps toward the window as if to be in deep thought.

JC: Where was I?

With a smile on his face, he turns toward me and continues…

JC: Oh, yes, one God and Israel. I was brought up in a time when rules and tradition were important. The mysteries of the universe were easily attributed to God. As well, the seemingly chaotic tragedies were also attributed to God. Too many times when one could not explain the reasons for a happening, the answer was simple: "It is God's Will."

At that time in history, we did not have the science that you have today. We did not have the means of communication that you have today. So, when something happened in a particular village, it was communicated and translated and passed on by word of mouth. People were much more naive, almost childlike, and that comment is not meant as a put down. Even today, humankind is still in its infancy.

Keep in mind that I was from the peasant class and the peasant class was basically illiterate. We could neither read nor write and totally relied on the temple elders and the leaders for guidance and the rules for living. The problem is that most people believed the 'stuff' they were told as the only truth, the only way to live. I was against any sort of unjustified killing or slavery, any injustice whatsoever. As long as people fear the unknown, judge difference and lust for power and control over others, they will not find the true meaning in what I was trying to teach. These people in power made up rules and myths to control the masses. They will say they were only trying to guide and moralize the people in order to help them to develop as righteous human beings.

When the Israelites needed to be strong and united they needed rules that were different than those of the other tribes. Rules that condemned and shunned the myths, mores and ideologies of those who would try to suppress, enslave or conquer the Israelites.

Me: The rules of the day were meant to say to the people of Israel that they should not do and believe in the things that the Romans or any other Gentiles believed in. This tactic was used to separate and solidify the Israelites, which was not necessarily a bad thing. Is that what I'm hearing you say?

JC: Yes, exactly. The problem is that the lawgivers and God inventors were obsessed with *their* concept of right and wrong; *their* idea of good and evil. God and the Devil went beyond common sense by creating a rigid way of thinking that did not allow for difference or deviance. And remember the word deviant simply means different from the norm. It does not mean wrong.

Me: Is that where you came in?

JC: Actually, I was what you might consider a deviant of the time. As I grew up I was challenging all I was told and all I saw. My parents, Mary and Joseph, were wonderful people. They allowed me the opportunity to grow and question. My need for answers sometimes became quite taxing to them. I remember my mother pointing her finger at me and saying, "Why can you not just for once stop questioning why you are doing what you are doing? The laws are specific. God is watching you and you shall be judged." Then she would give me that half little smile, that twinkle in her eye and pat my bottom as she pointed me toward the door and told me to go and help my father in the carpentry shop.

It's funny seeing him mimicking his mother as he relates the story.

Me: Anything written about your parents seemed to show them as wonderful people. If so, it must have been great to grow up with such understanding and caring people who allowed you to be the person you were meant to be.

JC: Yes, so true.

You could see his face light up as he talks about his parents.

JC: Joseph was a strong but gentle man who could do the most amazing things with wood. He put pure love into everything he did. And Mary, I cannot say enough about her. She carried me, loved me and nurtured me. And as you so aptly put it, they both allowed me to be the person I was meant to be.

The people who really had trouble with my constant questioning were my teachers and the temple elders. They used to force the laws and morals down my throat and when I said that I wanted to understand not just obey, they were quite upset. Many times I was told that that is the way things are, I had better get used to it and stop trying to rock the boat. The phrase, "It is God's Will," was the standard answer for all things. This really frustrated me yet motivated me to keep asking more and more questions.

Yes, my formative years were interesting to say the least. I understand that today you would describe what I had as Attention Deficit Disorder and prescribe a drug like Ritalin to help me conform more to the rules of the day.

He even knows about ADD and Ritalin. This is blowing my mind. But why did he have to bring this up? It really bugs me that the only answer to a child that is restless seems to be drugs.

Me: You had to bring that up didn't you? I get so incensed when I see our children treated so poorly. The system seems to reward mediocrity and punish creativity. I sometimes wonder how we have been able to evolve. Are you telling me that you were a problem child?

JC: Some would say that, but no, I was not a problem child. I was a curious child. I was actually obsessed with learning the truth. And when I say the *truth,* I mean the why and the how of who we are, how we live and why we do the things we do. We were all told by the elders what the truth was and were not given the opportunity to question that truth and that is a real problem. For you see if the truth can be questioned, discussed and argued over and over again, then I believe that the *real* truth will evolve. And what is truth for me may not be truth for you.

Me: Now *that* I understand and wish more people could grasp.

JC: It would make life a lot more bearable for many people. You see I was also quite concerned with the inequities of power that the truth holders used over the common people. Human dignity is something that is really important to me. I detest patriarchal power mongering, and I wanted to understand why people were so afraid of difference.

Me: I hear you loud and clear. That's the way I've always been and like you, people keep saying such things as, "That's the way it is, you can't change it." Or, "Why are you always trying to cause trouble?" Then they give you that look. You know ...

JC: Yes, I know that look.

He rolls his eyes upward and to the right and gives his head a shake.

JC: That look said, "OK, what is it now? What are you going to challenge or question? What rule do you think is out dated or just plain does not make sense?" Yes ... I know that look.

Me: I tell you it's sometimes so hard to challenge the rules. When we question our elders, it's taken as if we have committed treason or heresy. People who set down the laws and make the rules believe that the rules were meant to be respected and if they weren't needed, they wouldn't have been enacted in the first place. Age doesn't always equal wisdom.

JC: Tell me about it. All the time I was growing up, all I heard was, "Jesus, you must learn self control." "Jesus, do not bring forth God's wrath." "Jesus, people will not understand." And "Jesus, let it go, you cannot win if you go up against the lawgivers." And then when I got into my teens and early twenties, my family and friends were looking for me to settle down, continue with my career as a carpenter and find a mate.

Me: And why didn't you? You must've been under a lot of pressure.

JC: Yes. You have to remember that family and procreation were the two things that were uppermost in everyone's mind. Just look at the Ten Commandments and the morality laws. Do not get me wrong, at that time there had to be some sort of code of conduct. The people had to expand their numbers and those numbers had to be expanded among the Israelites, so therefore, other traditions and ways of being had to be shown as sin.

So here I was questioning everything. Trying to understand people and the way they interacted. I was very interested in the mind, thought and spirituality. You see, I was trying to find out what the true balance was between mind, body and spirit. The farthest thing from my mind was to settle down and have a family.

Me: I didn't seem to find anything written that actually talked about your early years and whether or not you had any relationships.

JC: Of course the Christian writers had to make my only love be the love of God and besides, I can see it now, "Son of God found in bed with so and so."

He smiles, for he seems pleased that he made a little joke.

JC: Sex and sexuality were pretty well repressed in those days. Sex *only* occurred between two married people of an opposite sex and *only* to procreate. And if you believe that, do I have a bridge to sell you. Besides, I truly was not that interested in a long-term relationship. I did my thing. Although I had a few short term relationships and some got pretty serious, I could not get past this little voice in the back of my mind that kept saying that a family and a traditional relationship was not in the cards for me. My true love was and still is humanity. As I said, I was obsessed with the balance between mind, body and spirit and that any type of repression is wrong.

I don't know if I should ask this, but I'm going to do it anyway.

Me: Are you telling me that you never had sex?

JC: I did not say that. As a matter of fact, the joy and the pleasures of love and sex ... no, not just sex but sensuality ... the true binding of two minds, two bodies and two spirits is the ultimate. I was talking about a life partner, a long-term relationship. I just had too much to accomplish.

Me: What do you mean, you had too much to accomplish?

JC: I knew if I could find the right balance of mind, body and spirit, I could accomplish just about anything that I put my mind to. If I found that key, a new spirituality if you will, and I could share it with others, I would be able to give people the power to change their lives. The power to get out from under the repression of Roman rule. And the power to challenge the restrictive right wing thinking of many of the temple elders. I believe if you have a strong spiritual belief, you will be able to attain peace of mind and peace of mind creates a healthy body.

I truly believe we can heal ourselves and I also believe *only we* complicate our lives and our relationships.

Me: Yes, I find it's generally not me who complicates things. It's all the people who go from either just having an opinion about my life to actually trying to control how I live my life. And why do these people feel the need to judge and moralize?

JC: We are still infants in this developmental journey of humankind and most people are frightened by what they do not understand. When no one knows for sure what actually happens on the other side, people tend to take the safe path. Think about it. Would you rather meet all of your ancestors in a heaven or burn in a hell?

Believe it or not, when someone is doing something different, it is difficult for people who need a sense of right and wrong, definitively defined, to justify as acceptable what they think is sinful. You see they believe if they accept that behaviour, they condone it. And if they condone it, they will burn in hell with the sinner. They do not understand that acceptance is not necessarily agreement.

That makes so much sense. I accept the fact that certain things have a right to be, but I don't have to agree or condone them.

JC: Let me put it another way. In order for a person to understand who he or she is, that person lays out a set of standards, rules or blueprints that describe exactly who that person is, what he or she stands for and how to live his or her life. Hence the Ten Commandments and moral codes. Therefore, anyone or anything that this person perceives comes into conflict with these ideals must be wrong, which makes him or her right. And if this person is right, then he or she is one with God and therefore will be blessed with eternal happiness and life.

Me: I understand why we must have rules and why we must have moral conduct. My problem, therefore is twofold. First, why can't there be simple basic rules for everyone to follow and second, if everyone is supposed to be right, then who in fact is wrong? You know, "My God is better than your God." Who is right and who is wrong?

JC: As I said, people perceive this journey in their own way. Some interact to contribute to the whole and some are destructive. To answer your first concern, there are such basic rules as "live and let live". Most of the animal kingdom understands this fact and do not kill or enslave for greed. And secondly, the interpretation of the various different God laws are to further some men's power base.

I was actually an egalitarian. I believe that all people should have equal political, social and economic rights. Some interpretations and writings of my life sent out a different message from the message I was really trying to pass on.

Me: You mean the Bible and the New Testament Gospels were wrong?

JC: Not wrong ... different.

I understand by his smile that he just made a great point.

JC: Remember what I said earlier. These books were written from the perspective of those present. In retelling stories or history, certain people emphasized certain points of view and when that gets passed on it has as much to do with how something is told, and what gets left out that affects what the next person perceives as truth. Even if you look at similar events in the gospels, they are seen, perceived and told to others with slightly different twists. And in some cases the twist is substantial. Also keep in mind that the gospels were written decades after my death.

Let me tell you some of the laws, customs and beliefs I had a problem with. First, let us look at God. How can God be all loving, all caring and all benevolent, yet that same loving, caring and benevolent God will crush and destroy all those who would disobey His laws? And this same loving, caring and benevolent God seems to endorse having innocent animals killed as a sacrifice to His greatness. Give me a break! That in no way represents my concept of a loving, caring God.

Now I have come along, according to the scriptures, to die for all the sins of mankind, so now if a person confesses his or her sins, they will be forgiven and all will be well. OK, you got the idea. In the Old Testament you sin, you die. In the New Testament you sin, repent, you go to heaven. And what gets me is that people actually believe this *stuff*. This is where I come in. As I reached my late twenties, I really started to question some things and I questioned these things in public, which frightened Rome and certain temple elders.

What kind of a God would want me to kill innocent lambs and pigeons to use as a sacrifice, then go as far as allowing some people the right to sell these sacrificial animals in the temple and profit from that kind of carnage? What kind of a God would allow some priests, elders and rabbis to get rich while they mentally, physically and sexually abuse and enslave the very people they were meant to serve? What kind of a God would proclaim certain people or animals "unclean"? These are the same people and animals that this God was supposed to have created.

He is supposed to be the Son of God. I can't believe he is saying these things.

Me: Those are some pretty strong words coming from the *Son of God* and a person who has a religion named after him.

JC: Let us get something straight right now. No pun intended.

He smiles and I can see a twinkle in his eye.

JC: Men who needed to use me for their own personal reasons created the *Son of God* thing and the religion thing. Yes, I had a following and yes, I had a message to deliver, but I tell you, that message has been misinterpreted, twisted and maligned over the years. It truly hurts me to see my name used in such a manner.

Wow, he makes a joke about using the word straight in front of a gay man, yet, I can sense that he is agitated. Maybe I asked the wrong question?

Me: I didn't mean to upset you.

JC: Do not worry, you did not upset me. It just irks me to think that I spent years fighting the power mongers, the users, the masters and the lawgivers only to find that the same type of people are using my name to do the same things today that I fought against two thousand years ago.

Me: Are you saying that you weren't the messiah, the saviour and that you did not die for our sins?

JC: I was actually what you would call today "a social activist," which was unheard of in those days. I was against repression. I was against slavery. I was against injustice. I was against the patriarchal hierarchy. I was against nonsensical ritual. And I was against discrimination of any kind. This attitude brought much attention to my life.

No, I did not die for the sins of man. I was executed because I was a social activist who was gathering momentum. I had a following and my main message was individual empowerment. I questioned Rome, the temple and the elders, the law and even God. This frightened people for I was saying and doing things that many people thought and wanted to do, but were too afraid to act upon.

I was totally in opposition to the self-righteous judgmental people of the time. They knew it and they were afraid.

Me: Fear can be a terrible thing. It makes people act in ways that can create much destruction and pain.

JC: Let's see, how do I put this in a simple and concise phrase?

As he looks out the window, he seems to be searching for the right words. He turns toward me and continues in a clear and steady tone ...

JC: I was a nonjudgmental egalitarian who believed that the individual had the power to control his or her own environment and therefore his or her own destiny.

His beliefs are very similar to mine. He truly understands the power within, but if he was in such control, how is it that he was executed?

Me: Look how much control you had. You allowed yourself to be executed in your early thirties.

JC: You are correct. But in fact I did have control. I could have kept quiet. I could have bowed to the power. I could have been a follower of blind faith and closed my eyes to all of the injustice, but I chose to take control of my journey and speak up. I chose to challenge and ask. I chose to share my vision with those who would listen, and I chose to stand by my convictions and I took responsibility for my own actions.

Me: But you were humiliated and killed. Wouldn't it have been better to live? Couldn't you have had more of an opportunity to change the system from within? For example, could you have not become an elder and help change the laws from the inside?

I've heard it said that the only way to break down the so-called "Old Boy's Club" is to join and break it down from the inside. You got killed and now the "Old Boy's Club" is using your name and God's name to maintain their power base. I don't mean to be rude, but it looks like you screwed up. You lost and they won.

Oh, oh, I just told Christ that he screwed up. But he doesn't seem to be upset.

JC: It could seem that way on the surface. But history has shown that many people truly did understand what I was about and they have contributed much to the dignity of humankind in my name.

Let me address what you said about becoming one of *them* and making change from within. That concept is much easier now but two thousand years ago I was a peasant who did not have access to the means to become upwardly mobile. A carpenter's son was to be a carpenter as was his father before him and his son after him. The only way to enact change was to empower the grass roots, the individual. I had to change the way people thought and how they lived their lives. And I truly believe I was beginning to accomplish that task. That is why I was such a threat and had to be discredited and removed.

Me: So how do you empower an individual? I know when I've tried to empower others, some people get it and change while others get it and are too comfortable to change. And there are some that'll never get it for they're too afraid of change. We're only here to deliver the message. It's up to the individual as to whether or not he or she accepts the message.

My own mother is a perfect example of the latter. She is addicted to pharmaceutical drugs, smokes heavily and after my father died, she totally broke down and has not been the same since. She constantly complains and is always sick. If it's not one thing, it's another. Yet I can see if she could only change her attitude, her perception of her life, if you will, how much happier she would be. It truly frustrates me to see a wonderful life so totally wasted.

I think perception is key to how you view your life and any situation that you're in. It reminds me of the story of the two little children who were put into a room for observation. The first child was put into a room full of expensive toys and games. This child was observed throwing the games and toys around the room while complaining and criticizing the type, construction and make of just about every toy. The second child was put in a room that was filled with about two feet of horse manure. This second child was seen searching through the manure and when asked, the child said, "With all of this horse shit around, there has to be a pony here somewhere."

JC: Heh, heh. That is quite good, not as good as most of my old parables, but still pretty good.

With a twinkle in his eye and a smile on his face he takes a small chair from under the window and places it a few feet from the window, turns, sits and faces me with both hands resting on his knees.

Me: I can see that you don't suffer from low self-esteem.

We both chuckle and you can see a bond is beginning to form between us.

JC: But that's my point. It is not about having a huge ego. It is about having a good sense of self along with a good attitude and positive perception of one's life and this journey.

It all comes back to the balance of mind, body and spirit. Each feeds the other. Without strong spirituality (and I am not talking about religion) the mind is weak. If the mind is weak, the body suffers. If the body suffers, the spirit is broken.

Me: What do you mean when you differentiate between religion and spirituality? I thought if you were a religious person, you were a spiritual person and vice versa.

JC: No, there is quite a difference between being spiritual and being religious. A religious person is not necessarily spiritual and the reverse is also true. Let me explain what I mean.

Me: Please.

JC: I consider myself spiritual and I know *this* will shock you, but not religious.

Religion in my mind is the belief in a structural ideology, a set of rules and mores of how to serve a God. Many people go to their temples or churches *religiously*. They obey the rules or laws that are set down by those who came before, usually without question and sometimes with a blind faith that creates fear in those who don't believe and shame when one's belief wanders.

This was as clear in the Mediterranean two thousand years ago as it is today. People, who are tied blindly to a particular religion and lack spirituality, use the religion and its rules to justify all sorts of atrocities that either they cannot explain or they themselves perpetrate in the name of their religion.

Now, a spiritual person understands the connection between all things, animate and inanimate, the oneness of mind, body, spirit and the planet. A spiritual person is comfortable with who she or he is and the part they play within this journey of organized chaos.

A spiritual person is nonjudgmental, for he or she accepts and actually celebrates difference. There is a clear understanding that difference is not necessarily bad, just different. These people also acknowledge that acceptance is not necessarily agreement. Many religious doctrines do not allow for this type of mindset. Their laws are absolute and they are taught to shun, not accept.

Me: I know that from experience. When I was in university, I became friendly with a few members of the university's Christian Fellowship Club. I used to have coffee with one person in particular and we have had many great discussions about life, politics and theology. He told me that he understood he had no right to judge me even though he felt my lifestyle was wrong. Interestingly he told me that some of his friends couldn't understand why he wanted to hang around a "known homosexual" and said if they saw us together in the halls of the school that they could not and would not say hello to him. In other words he was being shunned, but not because he was doing anything wrong, for he was totally straight, but is being shunned because he wouldn't shun me.

JC: You are right when you say that not much has changed over the past two thousand years.

Me: I know it seems that most religions haven't come into the twenty-first century. They seem to hang onto past laws with no way of adapting them to the changing and evolving world. It reminds me of the story of the young child who questioned his parent as to why the ends were cut off the roast when it came out of the oven. The parent said that she didn't know. She said that her mother taught her how to cook and always cut the ends off the roast. The child was told to ask her grandmother. When the child went to the grandmother, the child was chastised for asking such a question. The grandmother said that it was tradition and that she was taught the tradition from her mother and the child was told to ask her great-grandmother. When the question was asked of the great-grandmother, the great-grandmother looked at the child and said simply, "Well my dear, back in the old days, the pans were too small."

Again he smiles. It makes me feel good to know that he is so easy going. Too bad more people can't see and understand this side of him.

JC: Now *that* is an excellent story, and so true. You are an excellent storyteller. I sure could have used you two thousand years ago, for you see that is exactly what I was trying to accomplish. I was trying to get people to question, to ask why they were doing what they were doing.

There were many laws, traditions and ideologies that many people blindly followed in order to appease some so-called God. Frightened, superstitious people who had to find reason and meaning for their existence concocted many of those rules. Others made and enforced the rules to maintain their position of power.

Today, there is much technology available that answers many of these mysteries of the past and it is unfortunate that there are still some people who cling to unsubstantiated outdated ideologies.

I often thought of having "The One Law Society" and that one law would be, "Do Unto Others As You Would Have Them Do Unto You."

Me: One of your best and most wonderful sayings, and a statement that hasn't changed for over two thousand years.

JC: Thank you. It does have a nice ring to it. Just think how that would solve misplaced jealousy, greed and negative attitudes.

As he says this, he has this little smile in his eyes that tells me we are connecting more and more as we interact.

JC: Think about it. People should truly think about how their words and actions will affect others, and in fact they should consider how they themselves would feel if those words or actions were directed back at them. Think of how different many people's words or actions would be.

If I hit you, I feel the pain as well. If I steal from you, I lose an item myself. If I judge you, judgment falls upon me. If I cheat you, the same amount is lost by me. If I enslave you, I experience enslavement myself. By the same token, If I love you, I feel love. If I share with you, you will share with me, if I celebrate you, you will celebrate me. If I am honest with you, the truth will be known to me. And if I do not judge you, I shall not be judged.

As I have said time and time again, the power is within us. We choose how we react to a situation and we choose how we act in a situation. It is quite simple, if you are given too much change from a sales clerk, do you give it back or do you keep it? If you found a purse on the ground, do you empty it and throw it away or do you try to find the owner? Do you pass by one who is hurt, or like the Good Samaritan, do you stop and help? Keep in mind how you would feel if you were the recipient of certain words or actions.

If we look for the *why* in what we do or what we say, if we look at *why* certain rules, laws and mores are in existence one of two conclusions may be reached. Either the reason for the rule, law or more may no longer be valid, such as sacrificing lambs or pigeons on an altar to God. Or, the rule, law or more is truly understood, believed and embraced, for you have asked *why*. The *why* is clear and therefore it is then justifiable and valid for you.

Me: So you say that you were actually trying to get people to challenge the laws of the temple and Rome?

JC: It depends on what you would call *challenge*. True, I was looking to empower the people, especially the peasants, but I was not trying to cause rebellion or a takeover of the government or the temple. I wanted all classes to understand that change was possible and that change could be done peacefully and without violence.

You see, if someone who was perceived to have the knowledge or the authority told another of lesser status to eat camel dung, generally that person would eat no matter how distasteful it was. Similar to your story about cutting the ends off the roast, this would be done without question and therefore the abuse would continue generation upon generation. The interesting fact is the person giving the order to eat the camel dung is usually just following tradition and really does not know why the dung should be eaten. In most cases they honestly believe they are right in perpetrating the abuse.

All I was trying to do was to get people to ask and examine the reasoning behind their laws, rules and mores. And if both the giver of the rule and the receiver of the rule stopped and worked together with mutual love and respect in examining the rule, then change would in fact take place without revolution. But sadly that balance cannot occur because of both fear and/or greed.

Me: If I bring your concept into the present it relates to a belief I have as to why the youth of today seem to be rebelling more than in the past. My theory is this:

The youth of the past few generations didn't have the knowledge that the youth of today possess and if I can use your analogy of the camel dung ...

JC: Please do.

Me: When my generation or the generations before me were told to eat the dung, we ate it no matter what we thought or how we felt or how it affected us. Whereas today's generation has been brought up with access to more knowledge. Books, newspapers, television, movies and computers allow the youth of today a far greater base of knowledge and with that increase in information, the youth are simply saying, "I don't understand why I must eat this dung, please explain it to me."

The problem is that no one has yet been able to teach the previous generations how to answer the simple question of *why*. Believe it or not the first few times the *why* is asked, it's asked with respect. Yet all we hear as parents, lawgivers and church leaders is, *"WHY?"* "I question your judgment." "I question your father's judgment." Some of us even take it as an insult to ask, for we've been told that certain questions are taboo or heresy.

JC: You are so right, children are like sponges that do nothing but have the desire to soak up knowledge. The problem with some people in positions of power is that they understand that knowledge is power and that if they allow all of humankind to have knowledge then in fact the power brokers feel they will lose control.

Me: Are you telling me that the control freaks, the power mongers, the wife and child abusers and the bigots are all afraid of losing control?

JC: Generally speaking that is 100% correct. Try this: the parent creates a child, and while the child is in its infancy, it is totally dependent on the parent for its survival, this puts the parent in unconditional control. Now as the child amasses knowledge, the child may realize that he or she may not need the parent in the same way and that frightens the parent. So the parent, under the guise of protecting the child from harm, limits the information that the child is allowed to ingest in order to keep control over the child. The problem is that this type of control used to work in the past because knowledge was not easily obtainable. But today it is too easy for the child to obtain the knowledge and in some cases find out that they in fact have been deceived. The child then rebels and the parent loses control of the child, which is what the parent was trying to prevent in the first place.

Me: Can you give me an example of what you mean?

JC: Many parents and clergy seem to think of sex as one of the biggest taboos for young children and they do their best to keep the knowledge of sex and sexuality away from their children. Yet anyone who has ever had an orgasm ...

He just used the word orgasm. This I have to hear!

JC: ... or has been loved or fell in love knows that when done properly, it is the most amazing feeling that could ever be felt by anyone. And of course when a child starts to experience the orgasm, he or she gets confused. You see the child feels the wonder and cannot understand why that is so wrong.

I knew Christ would understand about sex and not see it as such a bad thing.

JC: The same holds true for love. Children are taught to love but not *that way*. The problem is that we are in fact sexual beings. Why do you think that sex was mentioned so much in the Bible? Sex and sexuality has always been part of our makeup and will always be part of our makeup. To hide it, repress it or condemn it is doing a great injustice to humankind. Sexual misuse and sexual abuse are about power issues and issues of low self-esteem. There is quite a difference between that and healthy consensual and loving sex.

Me: Hold on a minute, people are going to think that you are condoning sex with children.

JC: NO! ABSOLUTELY NOT!

That's the first time I heard him raise his voice. I must have hit a chord. He stands up and begins to walk back and forth as if to calm himself, then patiently makes his point.

JC: I am not talking about sex with children. I am talking about educating children so they understand and know what sex and sexuality is about. Do you want children walking around with wrong or lacking information on such an important topic? And there is no appropriate age to talk about this, each child must be treated individually, for each child matures differently.

He stops and looks at me quite intensely. I can see the passion in his eyes. I can see how much he cares about children and how he wants to empower them by making sure they have the knowledge they need to protect themselves.

JC: Think about this logically, most humans and especially children will go someplace when they are told not to. They will look into the box that says, "Do not open." When you put "restricted" on a movie, everyone wants to see it. It only makes sense that if sex is condemned, mystified and kept behind closed doors, everyone is going to want it.

Take Prohibition in the 1920s US. There was an outcry about the evils of drinking and how it is destroying the family. So with pressure from the right wing, the entire US became dry. The result was not that the consumption of alcohol stopped, or slowed down, in fact, it went underground. The other unique spin-off is that it fed organized crime and millions of tax dollars were lost. The same is true with sex and the sex trade. While prostitution is illegal, it will continue to support crime, drugs, disease and abuse.

Me: It sounds like you're in favour of decriminalizing prostitution?

JC: Well, why not? If prostitution is decriminalized, it could possibly be licensed and therefore, it can be made safe for all those involved. People who want to enter the profession will do so with a free will. And those who want to use the services of a prostitute will be able to do so in safety.

Me: I'm afraid it would be easy to misunderstand where you're coming from. It's not believable that you would condone such an action. It seems to be contrary to family values, which of course is what your name is being used to promote.

JC: Not that again. First of all, not everyone is in a relationship. Not everyone wants to marry or even *should* marry. And if the service is out in the open, it will be more difficult for people to sneak around to use it. Secondly, what two (or more) consenting knowledgeable adults wish to do as long as they are not harming others, is totally up to them.

The idea of sex between two married people, male and female, was only put forth in order to expand the population of the time. And the fact that most of the other tribes of the area condoned open sex and sexuality, it was again another way for the Israelites to stand apart and be different. It also helped to control the spread of disease, for the cures you have today did not exist.

Me: Hmm. Can we get back to your comment about teaching children about sex? Don't you think that children should be protected against such things? Don't you think they're too young to understand sex? And finally, one argument is that if you tell them about sex, they will want to do it and therefore we as a society will be promoting promiscuity.

JC: NO, NO, and absolutely not!

Oh, no, I did it again. He looks pretty agitated. Yet as quickly as it comes, the agitation seems to go. He takes a deep breath, looks me straight in the eye and calmly speaks.

JC: Please understand what I am saying. Sex is only one of the many taboos people have created to control others. I was only using sex as an example of how man has demonized something that in fact is innate and beautiful. My fundamental belief is education, not segregation. The more people, especially young people know, the more they are allowed to question, the more they will learn and the safer they will be. For they will have all the information to make informed and intelligent decisions.

Remember why we got onto this topic in the first place. Humankind must begin to share knowledge, all kinds of knowledge. Each person should be allowed to ask *why*, and he or she should be given an honest answer. There should be no question that would be considered taboo. If we are afraid to answer a question openly and honestly, just maybe it is the true answer we are trying to hide and *that* is what should be exposed in the first place.

Me: That type of honesty can be scary for people. It leaves them vulnerable and open to criticism. Many people are quite guarded about what type of information they share with others. I think they may feel that they will lose the upper hand and therefore could be taken advantage of ...

JC: Or their true agendas will be exposed and their power will be diminished.

Me: Hmm. You seem to have a real problem with some people having power over others. But, don't we need leaders and followers in order to have society grow and prosper?

JC: There is a difference between leaders and followers, and masters and slaves. I prefer to use the terms "knowledge givers" and "knowledge seekers." When the system is used properly, with ego and power eliminated, then the knowledge givers also are the knowledge seekers and vice versa. You see, this journey is about learning and sharing what you learn with others. It is much easier to pull a rope up a hill then it is to push that same rope up a hill. A good teacher, boss, parent or other, will get better results from working with, guiding and helping learners than from force, fear tactics or power mongering.

If you look at most of the problems in the world in the 20th century, they occur in countries where people are illiterate. Countries, whose people do not have the knowledge to know that they themselves have the power to create their own journey, are the countries where you generally see the problems. Most of these people do not know that they and they alone have the power to change their lives and the power to create their own destinies. That is what I meant when I said to create heaven on earth. The Kingdom of God is within. The peace and tranquillity one finds when one truly understands spirituality is the ultimate soul.

Are you beginning to understand what I was truly about?

Me: Yes. The picture is becoming clearer as we talk. However, my confusion still lies between the historic Jesus, the religious Jesus and your relationship with God. Is it as complicated as it seems?

JC: The writings about the historic Jesus and the religious Jesus are both strewn with accuracies as well as inaccuracies and exaggeration simply because, as I said before, they are based on people's interpretations and bias of the happenings of the time. Couple that with lack of technology, science and an over-reliance on superstition, myth and magic and you will get some distortions.

As for my relationship with God, I have to tell you that it is so simple, it is complicated. I repeat that I do not believe in the hateful, bias, discriminating, judgmental God that many fundamentalists of all religions or sects believe in. Moreover, I believe in a natural uncomplicated set of laws that create this organized chaos. I believe in the power of the mind. Call it "The Mind God," if you will. It is this "Mind God" that actually controls the destiny of humankind. The Mind God is the controller of thought. The Mind God creates our conception of who we are and what we can or cannot accomplish. We are what we think we are.

This is amazing. Is he saying that God is Us?

Me: Wait a minute. Hold on. Are you telling me that God is simply about mind over matter, that in fact all humans are God or part of God?

JC: Of course! How else could we have created the world we live in? Our Mind God creates everything. The question is, is there something out there that is controlling the Mind God, such as Allah or the Christian God? Or, is the Mind God "The God" and "The Only God"? Either could be true. Yet, if the Mind God is The Only God, then we humans are all God and we have created everything that has ever been created. This is what I was actually trying to share with my contemporaries some two thousand years ago.

You see, if God is within, then the answer to all things come from within, not from without. Our internal locus of control is the answer. The Kingdom of God is within. Heaven is here on earth, it is within all humankind to be Godlike and to create their own heaven here on earth.

This doesn't really make any sense to me. Why is this so-called Mind God creating bad things?

Me: Now I've got you, I think this concept is flawed, for if we do have this Mind God, then why is this Mind God letting us see and do destruction, not beauty and peace?

JC: Great question ...

My goodness, he is beaming, he seems to love a good discussion and seems to thrive on someone who asks the tough questions.

JC: You see the Mind God creates everything we need and the Mind God creates every perception and fear as well. For example when we needed answers to the *why's* of life, in the beginning when science and technology had not yet been created by the Mind God, our Mind God created the external gods to be the scapegoats for what we did not understand. These external gods were also the scapegoats for our own actions and phobias.

Me: Are you telling me that the God of Israel and the Christian God are these external gods that were created by your Mind God?

JC: Yes. My Mind God as you call it is the creator of all things. For the Mind God is pure thought and invention.

Me: So then Genesis and the creation of man is just a myth. Then where did we come from? How did we get here?

JC: Do you believe in infinity?

Me: Yes, I do.

JC: If you do then you will understand that we have always been here and we will always exist. There was no beginning and there will be no end. There will only be change. Evolution is fact. It is proven through science and technology. The only thing that we know for sure is that things change. This change has been measured over millions and millions of years. We are still infants in the process of the growth of humankind.

Me: If you use the term infant, then that means that we were at some point born and therefore were we not created?

JC: Not necessarily, our first consciousness is something that would be difficult to measure. When did that first humanoid become sentient? The evolution of humankind is a slow and painstaking process because as we have developed our consciousness, we developed all that goes with it. Rather than survive through instinct, we tend to question all aspects of life and when we want to justify our actions we create safe answers that alleviate our fear, guilt and responsibility.

Me: You're back to the Mind God again, aren't you?

JC: You got it, sport.

Boy, is he ever loosening up. Or, is it me that is loosening up?

JC: Humankind has always created everything we have and everything we know. The same humans have built cities and destroyed them. They have both loved and hated, saved and killed, all with the Mind God creating the perceptions with and without logic, depending on the human. Why is it that a spider frightens many, is a pet of some and dinner to others? Our personal Mind God creates these things and creates them differently depending on our individual life experience.

Me: Is that why you can have a family with two brothers and two sisters and each of them will turn out differently, even though they had the exact same upbringing?

JC: Yes, but I think we have to look at what you mean by the exact same upbringing.

Me: You know, the same set of parents, the same socioeconomic background, usually the same religion and the same schools. Why is it some drop out, some exceed and yet others are average? How does one family end up with a child who is a murderer and a child who is a priest?

JC: Let me first deal with your statement of, "exactly the same upbringing." Even though there are similar socioeconomic factors, similar schools and spiritual encounters, each child is dealt with slightly differently. It is those slight differences that are used by the Mind God to create that individual. It may be as simple as a parent giving a slightly bigger piece of cake to the first child than the piece that is given to the second child. The first child feels mildly superior, which could help to create a huge ego or create no concept of sharing. The second child could feel less loved and that could create greed or low self-esteem.

Also, each person's DNA has a set of circuits that reach to the external world and when one combines that unique physical makeup with a uniquely perceived experience, then that individual's Mind God creates that individual. Because of this, in some instances, a bad kid happens to good parents. However, because we are social beings we are all tied to one another in some form or another. That is why I have used the terms "organized chaos" and "do unto others"; for if we create ourselves from our experiences and our experiences are a result of reacting to the world around us, then we are all connected. All of our Mind Gods are helping to create the next moment, the next hour, the next day and therefore the next step in the evolution of humankind. Our problem is that we react to all of the wrong messages and we do not follow the natural laws, for we do not question when the little hairs on our necks stand up.

Me: I'm sorry, I don't get it, what do you mean about following the natural laws?

JC: Well, let us say that you are out with some friends and one of them throws a stone through a window of a vacant house. Then proceeds to say that all present must do the same or they shall be shunned. You know the act is wrong, yet in order to continue to be accepted by your peers, you throw the rock. You have contravened the natural law of "do unto others" in favour of the Mind God's created need to be accepted by your peers.

Me: I see, but why do we continue to do such things when we know it's wrong? It seems simple to me, that anything that purposely and adversely affects anything or anyone should not be done.

JC: I think much of it has to do with the need for most (if not all) humans to be validated. Many people fear rejection and therefore, they just want to have someone acknowledge their existence. They want to be loved and celebrated. The problem is in order to get that validation many will do just about anything to receive it. Therefore we will throw the stone through the window for no other reason than to be accepted by our peers. The concept of rejection or to be singled out as different is not something we are born with. I believe it is something we learn. Little children are like sponges, sucking up their environment. And that environment, along with preprogrammed DNA and the Mind God help to form the individual.

What I think is constant and what can create many problems is the strong emphasis on fitting in. The ideology that sameness is better than difference. When sameness becomes the rule, it is difficult to be different. In fact difference actually frightens some people. Yet the funny thing is, we all strive to want to be acknowledged and seen as different, but not too different.

Me: So you're saying that we want to be different and we want to be noticed and we want to be validated, but we don't want to stand out, take a chance and that we are afraid to be ridiculed as being too different? It seems to me as if we humans are trying to suck and blow at the same time. For instance, notice me, I'm different from you but don't tell me that I'm so different that I'm weird.

JC: Wait. Suck and blow at the same time?

Me: Well, you got the idea didn't you?

JC: Oh, yes, I got the idea. You know, I really like the way you express yourself. You are very visual.

Again I see the smile and the twinkle in his eye.

Me: You aren't so bad yourself. But I'm still trying to figure out how we get trapped into crushing difference instead of celebrating it.

JC: It all goes back to safety in sameness. For thousands of years we have been preached to about conforming to God's Plan or God's Will and if we deviate from what are considered the norms, we will reap God's Wrath. It has been the different people, the deviants of society who have looked at this journey differently that have helped society change and grow. Yet, every time a special human emerges, he or she has an uphill battle to try and be heard above the comfortable conformists.

Me: That's probably one of the reasons you were killed, because you were different, a nonconformist. As Kermit the Frog says, "It's not easy being green."

JC: What?

This is weird, he knows about Ritalin, ADD, and prohibition, yet he knows nothing of The Muppets. Dreams and visions can be strange. Well, that's the Mind God for you.

Me: Kermit the Frog! You know *The Muppets* ... TV ... Miss Piggy ...

JC: Kermit? Miss Piggy? Are these modern day Gods?

Me: No, just puppets used in a children's TV program. They actually teach some pretty good things about education and difference.

He must be playing with my head.

Me: But I'd like to explore this topic a little further. I have a concept about a group in society who has no sense of self. These people have been put on this planet to screw with our heads. They're the ones that seem to have a fair amount of control over the rest of us. They have a disease, it's called "anal cranial inversion" and frankly, because of this disease, these people have a shitty outlook on life. They mistrust, misuse, abuse and have no sense of *doing unto others.* Their idea is to *do it to others before others do it to them.*

I asked a local police officer what percentage of society will pick up a gun and shoot you no matter what the laws are and he said about 2%, so I call them my 2% society.

JC: Only 2%? You know, I sometimes think they must get together and travel in packs.

Me: It sometimes seems that way, but I think that many of these people are the followers of the 2%. Based on what you've just said, many of these followers just want to fit in and are afraid of the perceived power of the actual 2%. They feel they can't say no to the situation.

JC: Yes that is it. The 2%er is so loud and uses force to get his or her point across that it is difficult for most to comprehend that they themselves can change the outcome of the situation just by standing up to the 2%er. Some say that 10% of the people do 90% of the complaining.

Had people understood this concept when I was taken, tried and crucified, I might not have died at such a young age. And again, times were different then. I must restate what I said earlier, that the power to control this journey is within. Yes, most of the people turned on me and I was abandoned yet I truly understood why it happened.

The 2% as you aptly call them seem to be our testing mechanism. If the 2% did not foul up when they drink, we would not need alcohol laws. If the 2% did not steal, we would not need locks on our doors. If the 2% did not abuse children, we would not be afraid to hug a child. Yet when a 2%er acts up, causes an accident, rapes or kills, the entire community overreacts to the incident. We tend to overreact even more when our day is filled with many 2% situations.

Me: I know what you mean. For example, when I was the manager of a paint and wallpaper store, we had paint that guaranteed one-coat coverage. Well one day it seemed that every gallon of paint ever sold was being returned. So I started questioning the quality of the paint. I decided to check the returns to sales ratio and I quickly found out that in fact the returns were only about 3%. I soon realized that when I put the 3% into perspective it really wasn't that bad.

But, you must've been truly disappointed when so many turned their backs on you. Yet it was written that you asked God to forgive them, for they know not what they do.

JC: I understood something that truly helped me in my journey and aided me in dealing with all of the others who decided that their sole reason for living was to control me and my journey. You see I knew about my Mind God and I knew that my Mind God created my day. But I also knew that in a way I also controlled my Mind God. So I came up with this simple concept that allowed me to deal with your 2%ers.

People could physically hurt me. People could take away my belongings. They could even take my life, as you know they did. But they could never, never control or take over my mind, my soul, my spirit, my will or my essence. For I learned that nobody can hurt me but me. Did you get that? I cannot stress this enough. **Nobody can hurt me but me**.

*Did I get it? You bet! It makes so much sense. **Nobody can hurt me but me**. I and only I can control how I react to this journey.*

JC: When I came to this realization, that nobody can hurt me but me, I was able to shed or disregard any attack on my character or person. You see my Mind God made me strong. My Mind God said as a person who does not judge (and as you know, I do not judge others, for it is not my place) I therefore do not have to take to heart the judgment that people try to place on me.

So when your so-called 2%er tries to destroy me mentally or emotionally, my Mind God will not allow me to be hurt, for I know that I am a good person. I am a person of worth and I understand that the control of this journey is all within me. I will not allow a diseased person to ruin my day. I truly understand that I have an internal locus of control. How I react to the situation is the key, not the situation itself.

Me: Even though I understand what you're saying, my thought is that's easy for you to say. You're Jesus. You're the Christ. You can walk on water, heal the sick and feed the multitudes. You can do it all.

JC: But so can you …

So if I understand about the Mind God and don't let the 2% mindset take over my thinking, then I can achieve anything I want, similar to him.

JC: Every human has the ability to do anything they want, if they want it badly enough. Heroes, inventors, exceptional achievers, star athletes, award-winning performers and yes, even prophets and messiahs, are just ordinary people who have taken control over their own lives and not allowed the 2%ers to thwart their goals or to become 2%ers themselves.

Every person on earth has his or her own Mind God and every person on earth has the ability to create, to heal and to excel at whatever he or she chooses. They also have the ability to shed the yoke of slavery and repression. The ability to stand up and say, "No, I will not participate. You will not have control over me. I chose to be and do what I want to satisfy my needs in this life without losing sight of the needs of others and respecting their individual journeys."

Always remember, we are totally in control. We are the masters of our destinies. We command our own ship of life. Humankind complicates this journey. For example, if I was to give you an item and you refused to accept or take the item, then whose item would it be?

Me: Well, it would still be your item for I didn't take it. It would still belong to you.

JC: The same holds true with insults, put downs, judgments and any other type of mental, emotional or verbal abuse. If I do not accept the abuse; if I do not accept the words, then it is clear that the person sending the abuse still owns the abuse and it has been redirected back to him or her.

Me: So that old children's saying, "sticks and stones may break my bones, but names will never hurt me," is really quite valid and even powerful.

JC: Another good one, excellent! "Sticks and stones may break my bones, but names will never hurt me." Superb, that says it all.

Again, there's that smile of approval and that twinkle. I love it.

JC: During my trial by the temple elders, at my questioning in front of Pilot and the march through the city streets to my crucifixion, many truly terrible things were said, but I kept strong and I had my focus. I know I did my best and that I did nothing wrong.

If your quest is to improve the quality of life in others and while pursuing that quest you do not harm one group in favour of another, then you have accomplished the true goal of humankind. Keep in mind that the people most threatened by a person who desires that type of goal is a person who is afraid of losing power. They are afraid of losing their perceived identity, their position in society. What these people do not understand is that if all humans cooperate to elevate their quality of life, then *all* humans benefit, including the masters. Yet these small-minded people cannot see the benefit in keeping their so-called servants happy.

Respect is earned not legislated. For example if an owner understands that if the worker is treated with respect and dealt with fairly, which would include good wages and reasonable working conditions, the worker will want to do their best for the owner. By the same token, if the worker understands that the owner is allowed to and must have a good profit, the owner will be in a position to treat the worker better.

Can you see the circle? It is beautiful. Both the worker and the owner contribute to each other's quality of life. Therefore everyone benefits. Remember these keys, individual validation and self-empowerment.

Me: That all sounds well and good, but, in the real world people are greedy, they're selfish and they tend to covet what others have. How can I deal with the fact that if I leave myself open and vulnerable, someone will take advantage of me?

JC: Yes, it is difficult to reconcile putting yourself in a situation that will allow you to be taken advantage of.

Me: You know, "Once bitten, twice shy."

JC: There you go again ... "It's not easy being green" ... "Sticks and stones" ... and now, "once bitten, twice shy."

Me: Hey, it happens. I just seem to be able to remember some neat sayings.

JC: You certainly do. Let me expand on this last saying, "Once bitten, twice shy." It is good to be cautious and safe. It is good to be aware of the dangers that can lurk in the shadows. But, we cannot and should not allow the 2% to control our lives.

If a person or situation adversely affects me, I will be more cautious the next time I come in contact with that person or situation. The problem is humans tend to lump all similar people and situations in the same barrel. One Canaanite does something bad and all Canaanites are perceived as bad. "Once bitten, twice shy" should not mean that everyone is going to bite you.

Me: That's so true, but don't we take the negative in our lives and use that negative to protect our positions and control others? It seems to me that we tend to make mountains out of molehills.

JC: Again with the visuals! "Make a mountain out of a molehill." Does it ever stop?

Me: I couldn't help it. It just seems to happen.

Anyway, according to all accounts about your life, you constantly spoke in parables, didn't you?

JC: So they say ...

Another half smile comes over his face. He really seems to like the way we are bantering back and forth.

JC: But, let us get back to your "mountain and molehill." People do tend to overreact to situations and sometimes make things sound worse than they are, especially when people are afraid, because they lack knowledge of the truth of the situation. Our Mind God can have us perceive things to be worse than they are.

Let us say that we are making a movie of your life. Would this 'tragic event' be important enough to be included?

Remember, through constant seeking of knowledge and an ability to be nonjudgmental we can create a state of mind where we mitigate the escalation of the situation. In other words, the molehill is seen for exactly what it is, a molehill.

Me: But what if that molehill truly is a mountain and we dupe ourselves into thinking the situation less than it really is? Isn't that more dangerous than if we lull ourselves into a false sense of security?

JC: Overreacting and under-reacting can both create major problems in this journey. We must constantly feed the Mind God knowledge to give the Mind God enough information to form the proper state of mind that would be right for each individual. With the right mindset most situations do come into proper perspective.

Me: What do you consider a proper mindset?

JC: As I have already stated, there is an organized chaos out there that exists and there are natural laws that exist for the co-operative interaction of all things. It has been said, "our day is how it should be." We created this moment in time because of our perceptions and reactions to situations that occurred only a moment before. And because of a perceived bombardment of too much information, we become overwhelmed and try to control the outcome of the next moment. I think that sometimes our environment can seem to be too much for us.

Here is what I mean by proper mindset. We must understand a few basic principles of natural law and choice. If you stick your hand in fire you will get burned. If you venture outside in the freezing cold totally naked and stay out long enough, you will freeze to death. If you stand in front of a speeding vehicle and it runs you over, you will die. If you love, nurture and care for a dog, it will wag its tail and love you back. If you raise a stick and beat a dog, eventually, the dog will turn on you. If you protect yourself from the midday sun, you will not be burned. Most of these things we know. These are concepts of what I call the natural laws. We know these things to be true. There are the actions and there are the results of the actions. Generally speaking, love begets love and hate begets hate.

Once humankind evolved beyond instinct to reason, we began to complicate this simple journey and force change to the natural laws. In trying to understand why tragedies occur and how to avoid them, humankind had to place blame. I have already stated the Mind God created the external gods and myths to answer these questions. Yet the tragedies continue to occur even though the gods and myths have changed over time.

The only aspect of humanity that seems to have remained constant is the overreaction of some people to their situations and their need to control the natural laws in order to feel safe. The key is to learn how to let go and allow certain things to take their natural course. This going with the flow has to be coupled with a few other simple rules of conduct.

Me: And what would they be?

JC: First, one's mindset must be of trust and compassion. A person must trust that most people do not intend to do them harm and then compassion for those who do, for they are deeply troubled. Second, and coupled with the first is an old East Indian saying, "let only the good in me see only the good in you." By approaching all people and situations looking for the positive with a trusting and compassionate demeanour, you can not help but be rewarded. Remember to do unto others as you would have them do unto you will also result in the concept of reaping what you sow.

Me: See now you are doing it to me, "reap what you sow."

JC: I am allowed, remember, I am suppose to be the Messiah.

Me: OK Mr. Messiah, please continue.

JC: Mr. Messiah! Too formal, JC will do thank you.

Me: OK JC, please continue.

JC: Third, a person should be proactive instead of reactive. We do have the ability to control our day and that ability is coupled with what we did yesterday. You see most people get up in the morning and just let things happen to them. They react to the day and then they complain about the situation that they find themselves in.

Me: That's like the guy who goes into the doctor with a sore arm moves it up and down and says, "doctor, doctor, it hurts when I do this." The doctor says, "then don't do that."

JC: I like that. That is exactly what I am saying. We repeat situations in our lives simply because we are not proactive.

Me: OK, but what exactly do you mean by being proactive?

JC: Let me see … Ah, yes. Let us say that your partner is a neat freak and he likes to make sure that the dishes are done and put away right after the meal is finished. Let us then say that you are the type of person who takes his time to do the dishes. Sometimes it even takes hours before you get around to the dishes. Now this will tend to irritate your partner to no end. Knowing this, a proactive person would have made sure the dishes were at least rinsed and ready to wash. By the same token, if your partner were proactive, he would know that there is a possibility that those dishes would not be done as fast as he would like, and therefore could help you get at them instead of getting upset.

A proactive person will think outwardly and be totally in harmony with his or her environment. If you trip over a cord on the floor, either move it or tape it down so you will not trip over that cord again. That is proactive not reactive. A proactive person celebrates others and in turn is celebrated by others. A proactive person is usually not late for an appointment for she or he prepares ahead of time for little problems that could occur along the way. There are many different little bumps that show up in our journey everyday that will reoccur again.

A proactive person will do something today that will smooth out the bumps for tomorrow. A proactive person is safer than a reactive person because she or he has taken the time to make sure the machinery has been oiled and the ground has been prepared prior to the task at hand. As you said, "doctor, doctor, it hurts when I do this." "Then don't do that!"

Me: Oh, I see! Let me give you an example of how I think I'm proactive. When people drive to a large function at a hall, they usually fall in line and park behind the car that is in front of them. This happened to me once and when I got out of my car and began the long walk to the front door of the hall, I passed several vacant parking spaces along the way. So now I drive up to the front door and make my way back and, yes, usually I find a parking space near the front.

You also said something about letting go and I know what you mean about that as well. I seem to always find a parking space in front of the store or building that I need to go into because I don't put negative thoughts in my mind that there probably won't be a parking space. Even when I need some money to pay the bills, as long as I'm doing what is necessary to make a living, I know that the money will be there when I need it. I don't create unnecessary stress trying to control what will happen. I let go and usually it all works out. I think the problem is that we want things to work out one way and when they work out another way, we are disappointed in the outcome. Yet I know if I let go and allow for natural law to take over, it usually turns out for the best.

JC: Yes. For example, if you lose your job and you have trust and compassion for the situation along with being proactive in the sense that this could be an opportunity for positive change, believe it or not something better will come along.

The problem is we want instant satisfaction and on our terms instead of realizing that happiness is a state of mind. If we can see that this journey is what we make of it, we will truly have heaven here on earth. We are in control of this journey as long as we continue to be proactive instead of reactive.

Part of the reason we are here is to learn and when we learn from a situation so that it does not happen to us again in the same way, we become proactive. It is only when we keep making the same mistakes over and over again that we remain reactive.

Me: You mentioned the idea that we're here to learn. That's very interesting. We're here to learn what? And for what or who's purpose are we learning? Many people believe we're here to serve God and to help fulfil God's plan. My problem is that I have never felt like a slave in that I have to live for God and that I have to fulfil God's plan. If I believed in that theory, I would feel that I was being used and that would not make me happy. So, I'm interested in your "we are here to learn" concept.

JC: First of all the ideology that we are here to fulfil God's Will and God's Plan can be debated and maybe even challenged …

Me: You'd challenge God?

JC: No, not actually. Hear me out …

He raises both hands in the air as if to calm me down and listen to his explanation before I jump to a conclusion. He turns and sits back down in the chair, leans forward and continues …

JC: How do we actually know what God's Will or God's Plan truly is? All we know is what we have been told by man. All we are receiving is what man gives us. Remember it was supposedly a man that came down from the mountain with the Ten Commandments and told us he spoke to God. This man gave us some rules to live by and we believe them to be the word of God, not because we heard God ourselves, but because we believe that this man told us the truth. Do not misunderstand me, the Ten Commandments are a fine example of how humans should interact and coexist with mutual love and respect.

I have a real problem with the inconsistencies that man has created in God's Plan, God's Will and God's Law. Let us examine one of the Ten Commandments, "Thou Shalt Not Kill." On the surface it seems pretty clear, quite lofty and very simple. What seems to have happened over time is that "Thou Shalt Not Kill" has become "Thou Shalt Not Kill unless it is done in the name of God."

To me, this does not make much sense. I am given a commandment that seems specific. I am not to kill. Yet God can wipe out entire cities if He does not like how the inhabitants are acting. Clergy, in the name of God, can kill if they believe you are not acting in accordance with *their* interpretation of God's Will. Just look at the incredible carnage that occurred during the Spanish Inquisitions. Think of how many innocent animals and young virgins have been killed as sacrifices to God. No, I'm afraid God's Will is actually Man's Will and it is the will of a small group of men who only wish to control others and to protect their own positions of power.

He slaps both his hands on his knees as if to signify the completion of a thought and then says ...

JC: Now back to my comment about learning.

If we look at the evolution of humankind, we experience a situation, we overcome adversity and from this we grow. In terms of knowledge and understanding, think about how far we have come and how innocent we were in the past. We used to cover a baby's face when the baby yawned because we thought that the baby's life soul would escape. Today we know differently, yet we still cover our mouths when we yawn, not because we are afraid of the life soul escaping. We now say it is polite.

In the past it was common practice to bleed people as a treatment for many illnesses, today we know better. The more we learn the more we grow, the more we grow the more we mature and as we mature, we shed old superstitions and myths that we know to be false or ineffective.

The problem is many people still cling to the past and are reluctant to look at something new because new is frightening. Sometimes these people who are afraid of change actually stop learning. When they stop learning and are comfortable with only what they know, they get complacent and actually hamper change. These people see change, not for good, but as a disruption of the norm. What is that saying, "Better the devil we know than the devil we don't."

Me: Yes, people are afraid of change. They are afraid of difference. Is that human nature or has it been bred into us?

JC: I believe it is a learned behaviour. Let me repeat what I have said about the past. People were compelled to believe that there was only one way to think and only one system to believe in. If they deviated from that, they would burn in hell. The wrath of God would come down on them from above. Even today as I have pointed out, we mold our children to fit into what we as adults believe is proper and we discourage anything that could be seen as different.

We must understand that learning and looking at life differently is not wrong. Having different beliefs will not result in the destruction of humankind. We must begin to understand that as we learn we grow and as we grow we see that difference is not bad or sinful. You know what is really interesting is that as we become more and more secular, we become more and more accepting of difference and more tolerant of others, for we are not caught up in the religious dogma that can create segregation and hate.

Me: There you go again, dissing religion.

JC: Dissing? What does that mean?

Me: Oh, it means to put something down or to insult it.

JC: What I have said is not a put down, it is fact. If we look at the history of religion, we see that there must be an enemy without in order to control and keep the people within.

Me: It's not only religion that does that. In the old days tribes and villages did the same and today, many nations seem to always have enemies to worry and complain about. It almost seems to bring people together if they're fighting a common enemy.

JC: So true, and you are correct. It is not only religions that create the enemy, it seems to be true with nations as well. Remember it was the nation of Israel that created "the one God theory" to separate them from the other tribes in the area, resulting in the ideology that anything that was not part of the law of Israel was wrong.

Me: Come to think of it, it almost seems like human nature to create a "them" against "us" mentality, doesn't it?

JC: Yes, it does. But is it human nature or have we been doing so for so long that we actually believe it to be innate?

I truly believe that we can change this type of thinking. In fact, that is what I was trying to preach before my untimely death. There need not be an enemy without. All we need to do is conquer the enemy within.

Me: What do you mean by the enemy within?

JC: When we are educated and we learn, we are able to overcome this enemy within.

Take the example of a small child that has been frightened by a barking dog. The parent calms the child down. Takes the child over to the dog and shows the child that the dog's barking is how this animal communicates. The parent has the child pet the dog and also shows the child how to approach a barking dog, slowly and easily. The child is taught that the dog is probably more afraid of the child than the child is of the dog.

Through education and learning, the child sees that he or she can coexist with the dog. You see the enemy within has been conquered. Unlike in the past, the power brokers might say that this type of dog is evil and show the barking as a threat thus creating an enemy within which segregates the child from the dog. It pits the two against each other and creates hate and mistrust.

Me: That type of thing still happens today. Just look at the Arabs and the Jews, the Irish Catholics and the Protestants, the Christians and the Muslims, and I could go on and on.

JC: Unfortunately, you could. I tend to wonder when humankind will finally understand that we are all one. We are all citizens of the world. Every religion and every God comes from the same place. They all come from the Mind God. If we look at most religions of the world, the basic ideology is love and respect. However, some people in power in these religions feel that there must be that enemy without to keep the flocks together.

Most ordinary people in these religions and nations do not want to fight. They are just trying to survive, just trying to feed their families and just trying to do what is right. The problem is that people who would have them hate, instead of love, will actually lead them down the path of destruction.

Me: Why?

JC: The answer is simple: power and control. Look at it this way, if I had a position of power and respect in a community that kept my family and myself in the limelight, would you not think that I would do anything I could to protect my position?

Me: Even to the point of lying, cheating or murder?

JC: Even to that extent. And do you know what is even sadder, is that these people come to believe with all their hearts that they are right. That they are doing these things in the best interest of their family and the people they govern or preach to.

Me: Oh, come on. I can't believe that!

JC: Truly. Even the people who had a hand in my death honestly believed that they were right. The enemy within created me as the enemy without. Sometimes we get caught up in the mentality of the group and we do not seem to question the group or see the stupidity of the masses.

Me: I'm having a real hard time with this. Are you telling me that people like Hitler, Saddam Hussein, Pilot or Herod can be compared to overprotective parents or the overzealous pastor?

JC: Not one hundred percent of the time. There are *some* truly evil people, but I *do* believe that even these people started out basically good. Because of their own weaknesses, their enemies within, their need for validation, they chose a path that at first did not seem harmful, but turned out to harm others.

I do not want you to feel that I am associating the overprotective parent or the overzealous pastor with a type like Hitler, but I do believe that all of these people began their journey with a basic belief that they were right and their actions were justifiable. But because of their need to be validated and their taste for power, they get to the point where the need to stay in control outweighs the common good. Some people in power become so blinded by the need to stay in power that they begin to believe their own lies.

Let us say, hypothetically, that the Pope discovered indisputable evidence that there is no God and that I am not in fact the Son of God. Do you think that this pious, God-loving, people-caring man would tell the truth and throw out everything that his people have fought for and built up for thousands of years? I think not. He could not do it and there are very few of us that could do it. For those of us who have dared to challenge the status quo, we have been and are dealt with swiftly and permanently. And as in my case, my name and my life are being used to perpetuate many falsehoods.

This is incredible stuff. Did I just hear Jesus say that the Pope would cover-up the nonexistence of God if in fact that is the truth?

Me: Hold it. Let me catch my breath. Are you saying that we'll never know if evidence was found to dispute the existence of God and you as saviour?

JC: Unless a secular thinking anthropologist of today finds indisputable evidence that God does not exist, it will not happen. I believe that any evidence that did exist has either been destroyed or guarded so well that the general public will never know what really happened in the past.

Me: Hmm. Just like *The Planet of the Apes.*

JC: *Planet of the Apes?*

Oh, no, not again. I thought he knew everything, but it seems he knows some history, but not much about TV or movies.

Me: Yes, it was a movie that depicted apes ruling the world. They talked and thought and dressed. They had a government and an army. Humans were slaves and used for experiments. The apes also used humans as museum displays. It was most interesting to see humans being treated as animals by animals. The apes considered the humans inferior.

The leaders of these apes knew the secret of the past and did their best to hide it from the general ape population. They made up their own myths of creation and domination.

JC: What was the truth they were hiding?

Me: The truth in the movie was that the humans had destroyed civilization as we know it and that apes evolved to be the dominant species. If any human showed signs of intelligence, he or she was destroyed for fear of an uprising.

JC: That is exactly what I have been talking about. And because "the keeper of the keys" will not let us into the room, we only know what we are told. Unless we begin to question what does not make sense to us, we will remain slaves to myths and beliefs that do more harm than good.

Me: Is that what you were looking for and preaching about in the past?

JC: Yes, in a way. I was trying to tell people that they had the power to control their own lives and that the answers to many of their problems and questions could come from within. Now this enraged the temple elders and the Romans, for it challenged the rules that the lawgivers gave to the people. Being uneducated and frightened is one thing, but being educated, in power and frightened is just plain dangerous.

Me: You keep bringing up this fear thing. It almost sounds like most of the human atrocities came about through fear, not greed, power or evil.

JC: If you analyze the reasons we kill, lie, cheat and steal, it is because we are afraid of the other person and what we think that other person can do to us. Some people with power are afraid they are going to lose their power. Some people with status are afraid they are going to lose their status. Some people in control are afraid they are going to lose control. As well, some people who strike out in anger do so because they do not have power, control or status and are jealous of those who do.

Anyone who tries to control any relationship is doing so because they are afraid that they are going to lose that relationship.

Poor people steal because they are afraid that they are going to starve. Even the gang member steals because they are afraid they are going to be shunned from the gang.

Maybe that is why fear was and still is used to control the masses. If people think that burning in a hell is worse than eating the apple, they may not eat the apple.

Me: Hmm, eating the apple was the original sin.

JC: Yes, the original sin. The basis some Christian religions use to say that all of us are sinners and that we had our chance and now all of our actions must be to atone for that original sin.

Me: And then, of course, you were sent down to die for our sins and then you rose from the dead to show us that we can live again.

JC: Something like that. The concept is fascinating. You see no one can really prove anything different. It was written in the Bible and therefore it must be true. There were witnesses who said that they actually saw me with the nail marks in my hands and feet.

Well, I guess I have to know and I should just come out and ask the question. I don't know if I'm ready for the answer, but here goes.

Me: I have to ask. Did you actually rise from the dead?

JC: I was wondering how long it would take you to ask that question. If I answer, yes, I will perpetuate the myth about me and God and Christianity. If I say no, I will dash the hopes of millions of believers that there is a better life than the one they were dealt. If I do not answer the question, you will probably pester me until I do.

Me: Of course, I will. You *could* stall until I wake up from this dream and then I'd never find out.

JC: OK. OK. Did I really rise from the grave? That is the question right?

Me: Right, can you give me the answer, please?

JC: I will do my best. To be honest with you, I do not really know if I actually rose from the dead or not.

Me: See, I didn't think you'd be able to give me the answer.

JC: You misunderstand. It is not that I do not want to give you an answer, it is because I truly do not know for sure. You see it is similar to when we sleep. We go into another dimension and when we go from one dimension to another, we do not necessarily remember the occurrences of the other dimension.

When we dream, we believe that we are truly experiencing the event. And unless we train our minds to remember the dream, we usually forget it within the hour of our awakening. Also, when we are asleep we do not experience what is transpiring around us in what we would call the present. During sleep it is as if time stood still or sped up. Think about it, when we are in a deep sound sleep, we have no sense of real time, we are in dream time and when we are awake, we have no sense of dream time or dream space.

This is also true with visions. A vision is only experiencing another dimension. With some of us the visions are clear and real, while with others they are quick and ambiguous. Some say dreams and visions tell us what we need to know. That in fact, the other dimension is sharing the wisdom of the ages with those whom will listen and for those who will interpret the vision or dream.

Now I'm really confused.

Me: Are you saying that those who witnessed your resurrection had a dream or vision? And if so, how could two or more people experience the same vision?

JC: There have been cases over the years of mass hypnosis or visions. The mind is a strange thing.

By the way, I am not saying that these people had a dream or vision and I am not saying that I actually rose from the dead, for I have no recollection of the resurrection. That is not to say it did or did not happen. Just as this conversation we are having is very real to you at this moment and you may remember most or all of it tomorrow, I will not, for I will have gone back to pure energy. I will be in another dimension.

Me: Can you tell me what it is like in that other dimension?

JC: Not really. All I can remember is that it is pure energy. There really is no sense of time, space or matter. I know there is existence and there is this amazing sense of peace, love and knowledge, but even that seems quite vague to me when I am here in this manifested state.

Me: Do you believe there is a heaven and a hell?

JC: I doubt that there is, for I believe when your energy force (or as some would call it; the soul or life force) leaves the body, it takes all of its experience and knowledge with it and all of that joins to the energy of the ages.

Me: I thought you said you didn't know what happens after death.

JC: True. I have only stated that I believe this to be the way it is. I do not know for sure, for I am here at this moment and it is there. I only know that I have a strong feeling that what I have said could be true.

Me: So there is a possibility that there is life after death?

JC: Sort of, but not as we perceive life and death. I believe that we actually go from energy to matter and matter to energy, not dust to dust or ashes to ashes.

Me: This really gives one something to think about. That could mean that we have always been here in some form or another and we will always continue to be here in one form or another. If our energy lives on, we in fact never die.

JC: Yes, you could look at it that way. Remember our earlier conversation about infinity?

Me: Yes.

JC: Well, I think that you just figured it out.

Me: Let me see if I understand what you've said so far.

I pause and take a deep breath.

Me: The only true God is the Mind God for the Mind God has created everything we know, everything we have, everything we are and everything we were.

JC: Yes.

Me: So this Mind God even created the history of our existence.

JC: That is correct.

Me: And we go from energy to matter and back to energy again.

JC: Good. Please continue.

Me: And whatever we need comes to us from this vast energy field in the form of prophecies, visions and dreams.

JC: You listen well.

Me: But …

JC: I was waiting for the "but."

A huge smile comes across his face and he begins to laugh. I laugh along with him.

Me: Ha, ha. But, why are there people who have had visions of doom and death, prophecies of Armageddon and nightmares of destruction? Not to mention the people who predict earthquakes and in fact the earthquake actually happens. How much does nature have to do with the Mind God?

JC: Keep in mind what I have said. We get what we need from the energy field and we get what we are looking for, as all of the answers are out there. Therefore if someone is connected to the energy force, this person could in fact predict the earthquake.

Let me see if I can explain the difference between the binary opposites of good and evil, love and hate, construction and destruction, and even heaven and hell.

We are what we think and believe, and this positive or negative energy attaches itself to our persona and radiates outward to affect others. That is why animals and young children take to some people and are afraid of others.

Me: Yes, it's said that animals can sense fear.

JC: Not only do they sense fear, they sense aggression, submission and love. All emanate from the Mind God through our bodies and from our aura that creates the nonverbal communication that many of us do not acknowledge, because we cannot see it and unless we learn how to use it, we miss the message.

Even though animals and plants cannot speak as we speak, they do understand much more than humans do, for they tap into the pure energy of the life soul. It is like reading the mind.

Me: So if I learn to project a positive, loving and caring energy force, my life will be perfect and I will find heaven here on earth.

JC: Pretty much, but ...

Me: Now you're "butting" me ...

JC: Funny. But, it is not that simple, for we must interact on a daily basis with all of the other various forms of energy that are out there. These energy forces either add to or take away from our journey.

At our present evolution in history, keeping in mind we are still infants, we are still developing and learning how to coexist in this world of organized chaos. And, I truly believe as more and more humans develop their sense of positive energy, the realization that love conquers all, one day when all humankind understands the concept of positive love energy that flows through us into the world, there will be peace on earth.

Me: I've a feeling that time is not just around the corner. I think we have a long way to go.

JC: It does seem that way and there have been times in the history of humankind where the world appeared to consume itself with hate. But each time that happens the overriding love that exists in the entire energy force turns the tide and we move on to better times with more understanding and knowledge about the world around us and the people in it.

Me: So, if I think evil thoughts and if I look for trouble, then the Mind God will show me how to find it. By the same token, if I feel love and look for the good in all people and all situations, generally speaking, I will find joy and happiness or heaven on earth.

JC: Yes! That is it!

Boy is he excited. Like a child who just discovered a treasure. He jumps up from the chair and claps his hands together as if to applaud this new discovery.

JC: That is all I was trying to say, but because we were such children back then and because we were slaves to rules, myths and the whims of the lawgivers, I was seen as a threat to the status quo and had to be eliminated.

Me: That must've made you feel really sad and hurt to think that so many turned against you when all you were trying to do was to show people how they could empower themselves to break the mental chains that bound them.

JC: Yes, I was sad and hurt.

I have this overwhelming urge to hug him. But can I? Should I? We've been talking about feeling the energy force and acting upon the positives instead of the negatives. This is a positive and therefore I should and must act upon it before the moment has passed and it'll have been too late.

Me: May I give you a hug?

He seems surprised, yet pleased.

JC: Yes, a hug would be most appreciated.

I rise from my bed and slowly walk over to where JC is standing with his arms outstretched. As I come close I can feel an immense surge of love energy. I have never experienced anything so powerful.

We embrace and I'm consumed with love. Consumed with unconditional positive all encompassing love. We hold each other for what seems like an eternity. The experience brings tears to my eyes and a feeling of total safety. While I'm in JC's arms, nothing or no one can harm me. The love energy is so powerful that any misgivings, hate or hurt that I have seems to drain from my body as if being sucked out by a powerful vacuum.

JC slowly moves his arms from around me and holds me by my upper arms and looks directly into my eyes and as I look into his eyes I too notice tears running down his face onto his beard. Then he cups the sides of my face in his hands (I am melting) and stares at me for a moment ...

JC: That was incredible. Thank you. Your energy is wonderful. It felt really good to hold another man again. To touch and be touched and to love and be loved is the ultimate in this dimension. People who are afraid to hug and love are truly missing one of the primary reasons for being.

As his hands move from my face back to my shoulders and along my arms to my hands, he stands back gently holding my hands in his ...

JC: Is there anything else I can do for you while I am here?

Me: Actually, if you're not in a hurry, there are some more questions that I'd like answers to.

JC: I am yours until you decide otherwise, for this is your vision and your Mind God will guide you.

Me: Good, please come over here and sit with me on the bed.

JC: Thank you, that would be nice.

We move over to the bed and sit facing each other with our legs curled up under ourselves. It's as if we're two best friends having a sleep-over, sharing the deepest secrets of our souls and solving all the problems of the universe. There is a bond.

JC: So, my friend, what can I help you with?

Me: You certainly have clarified much for me. Your philosophies and your concepts of the Mind God and the energy force make so much sense. I'd like to bring your thinking into the 21st century to see how it would apply to present day circumstances.

JC: It sounds like you have quite a list.

Me: I certainly do. Sometimes I think the human race is really screwed up. And it seems to me that religion has a huge part to play in that screw up.

JC: First of all you must remember that all religions are man-made. And depending on the mindset of the leadership, each religion has the potential to become its own worst enemy.

There is an old saying, "The fish rots from the head." The head of the family, the head of the church, the head of the village, the head of the school, the head of the nation and most important is the head of the individual all determine the health of the rest of the body. This body can be the person themselves, the family members, or the congregation. The body can also be the citizens of the village, nation or the students in the school.

People must understand that they are in control of their own destiny. If they do not like the direction the head is going in, they have the power and ability to make change. I was but only one person and look at the change that resulted in my social activism.

Me: I have to say you certainly did have an impact on humankind.

JC: Thank you. Although I am not proud of the atrocities that have been done to others in my name, I have to say many, many people truly understood where I was coming from.

Me: And that leads me to a specific question that has been on my mind for years. What do you think of homosexuality?

My problem is that people use the Bible and your teachings to condemn same-sex relationships, saying that it is clearly against God's Plan for man. They say that God created Adam and Eve, not Adam and Steve.

He starts to laugh.

JC: That is funny. They actually say that? How childish and immature to suggest that their God would only create what they would consider appropriate.

This further supports my belief that there is much that has been misinterpreted about the Bible and what actually transpired during and before my time on earth.

Let me say that there is absolutely nothing wrong with consensual intimate love between two people. And as I have demonstrated many times, no one, absolutely no one has the right to judge what others do, as long as no one is being adversely affected by the action.

Back in my time we did have people who were what you call homosexual. We did not have a word for this kind of love, for when someone tells you that homosexual love is forbidden in the Bible, they are wrong. The word homosexual was not even invented until the 1860s, therefore it could not have been a taboo. And as for God's Plan, which they assume to be that man should go forth and multiply, *that plan*, as far as I can see, is still being fulfilled. The population is not suffering because some opposite sex couples choose not to have children, or that some heterosexual people choose to stay single, or that gay or lesbian couples choose to be the people they were meant to be, fall in love and live together. Of course even back then there were the few who had to make an issue out of the fact that these people were not contributing to the expansion of the population. Every generation will have some that are afraid of difference, this I have already dealt with.

When two people truly love each other and that love comes from the heart, is pure and consensual, no one should tamper with it. Obviously, I am not talking about rape or the use of power, such as an adult with a child, that is *not* love and it is *not* consensual.

Me: Some people today are saying that if you accept Jesus as your saviour and you follow his teachings, that you should be against homosexual relationships and that a homosexual relationship is a sin.

JC: I would never have suggested such a thing then and I would not now. For two people to find unconditional, consensual, pure love cannot be sinful and should not be taken as such.

I knew it. I knew Jesus would not and in fact could not have a problem with homosexuality. So I can be Christian and gay. I must get further clarification.

Me: These people who condemn this type of behaviour say that it's a choice and like alcoholism, it's a disease that should be cured.

JC: Were that true, then it would also mean that most of the animal kingdom is sick and should be cured, for as you know, many animals have sex with the same gender. If we take this thinking to its fullest, how is it that animals, who only act on instinct, seem to do quite well in the procreation department and still manage to have same-sex relationships?

Me: These people would say to you that we are above the animal and should not do what the animal does.

JC: Just as the old laws of paying for and sacrificing innocent little animals to God were, in my mind totally ridiculous, I believe this is another example of fundamentalist type thinking that creates an enemy without in order to control the people within.

Me: So you don't have a problem with consensual same-sex relationships, or as the fundamentalist would say, "the homosexual lifestyle."

JC: First of all, I do not have the right to judge the actions of others and secondly, how can anyone, especially me, have problems with love, for I am pure, unconditional love.

Besides, it would be a greater sin to force someone to do something that would be against his or her nature. How would the heterosexual like to be forced to become homosexual against his or her will? This would also be a sin. As far as I am concerned, the ultimate sin would be not to be the person you were meant to be whether that is homosexual or heterosexual. Too many people deny the true essence of who they are in order to fit into the narrow mold that the church, the lawgivers or some friends and family have concocted.

Me: You can't imagine how much pain the church has caused gay people over the years. It boggles my mind when I read about churches that condemn love.

I find it hypocritical when I read in the papers that the Christians are being persecuted in Muslim countries. They say they feel like second-class citizens, that all they want is to be treated as equals and be able to practice their religion in peace. And I'm sure that the Muslims living in Christian countries are saying the same thing. However, those same people will then make representations to government officials not to allow us gay and lesbian people equal rights for our relationships. They persecute us in the exact same way they are being persecuted by others.

JC: I will say this now and I will be quite clear. No religion, no government, no institution and no person in the world has the right to discriminate against those who do not share their beliefs. They have a right to their beliefs, no matter what they may be, but only as long as those beliefs do not judge or harm others.

The rule in your house may be to not wear a hat indoors and you have the right to enforce that rule for anyone who chooses to enter your house. However, you do *not* have the right to tell me that I must take my hat off in my house.

Me: How did you know that I have this thing about wearing a hat? It has become my logo.

JC: Remember, I know much about you, for I am in fact in your vision and have been created by your Mind God.

Me: OK, then following the logic of the hat example and relating it to homosexuality, some would say that their freedom of religion should be supported and they shouldn't have to allow gay people into their house.

JC: I believe the argument comes down to who controls the public space and who controls the private space.

Public space should and must be shared by all humankind. It is only good manners to coexist in mutual respect of all living creatures. The animal kingdom does this quite well. Just look at how all creatures coexist with mutual respect for space. One animal would never think of killing another simply because of their breed, their sexual orientation, or their eating habits. Yet how many times has one human killed another simply because they did not like the way they were looked at?

Private space is different. If I do not want you to wear your hat in my house, my house rules should be respected, or you do not have to enter my house. By the same token if I buy up all of the houses in order to make sure that hats are banned from existence, this is wrong. For I am now adversely affecting others in the public space.

Do not let these people use the freedom of speech excuse to hide the fact that all they really want to do is to control others and put their beliefs forth as the only true beliefs.

Me: What really bothers me is if I knew someone was using my name to do harm to others, I would do everything I could to stop them. Why don't you and/or God do something about those who use your house and name to do harm?

JC: The simple answer is that we cannot do a thing. First of all you must remember that man's Mind God created God and only the Mind God can do anything about anything. Secondly, I am only energy now and it would be impossible for me to do anything in this day and age. I existed long ago and today I only exist as a creation of what is written and what is believed.

It is up to individuals to reach deep into their own hearts, look at the situation and ask themselves, "what would Jesus do if he were here right now"? The pure of heart will do the right thing and the people whose Mind God shows them fear and the need for power will still continue on their path of destruction.

Me: How does someone stop this abuse?

JC: It is not a simple thing to go against the power brokers, but it is possible to make change and to take humankind to its next level of development. It must be done with love and compassion. It must be done with the understanding that all people have the right to coexist on this planet as long as their actions do not adversely affect anyone or anything.

Speak and write about unconditional love in the media, point out injustices to your peer group, stop violent controlling behaviour in families and most important of all, be a role model for unconditional love and compassion to all humankind.

Me: That sounds good and I do try to be that example. But I have to tell you that it's so difficult to maintain that sense of peace when all around you there's abuse and suffering. My next question is, "Why does it seem that good people suffer and bad people seem to prosper?"

JC: Remember I suggested that we are manifest in human form from the energy force in order to learn.

Me: Yes.

JC: Well, I truly believe that learning is the key. What I really do not have an answer for is why certain events happen to certain people. Why does an innocent child die at birth? Why do people get sick and die? Why do the "Hitlers" of history seem to get away with what they do? Maybe I can explain it in a way that might bring some order to the *why*.

Every living organism seems to have a cycle of birth, life and death and in many cases rebirth will follow in some form or another. Even though each organism appears to be different and independent, each organism is actually connected or dependent on each other.

Each organism works to maintain the whole yet is independent in its personal development. Let me give you a few examples of what I mean.

Take for example, a plant or a tree. A seed is germinated, it is given sustenance and it grows. It is affected by the elements: the wind, rain, heat and cold. Usually, it lives and flourishes, goes through a full life cycle and produces more seeds to perpetuate its kind. And some flourish more than others depending on their individual makeup and the circumstances of change.

Some are stepped on and some are picked at random, while others are cultivated and harvested in order to sustain another organism.

Me: "Organism" sounds so impersonal, so clinical.

JC: In a way, I want you to think in that manner. Not so you will be devoid of feelings, but to have you realize that in this organized chaos, whatever happens to us is not personal.

In our arrogance as humans, we think that we are the centre of the universe. We believe we are the most intelligent organism that exists. That is totally incorrect. Yes, we are different. Yes, we have evolved to the point where we have accomplished much. But we are still developing and we still have much to learn.

Maybe like the plant that was stepped on, the tree that was cut down and sacrificed as a decoration for Christmas, the squirrel that was hit by a car, or the spider that just happened to be in the wrong place at the wrong time, it is not personal.

Each time one of these events occur, do surviving plants, trees, squirrels and spiders sit around saying, "poor me," "why did this happen," or does the cycle just simply continue? And does the plant not feed another organism? Does the decorated tree not provide employment to the organism that makes the decorations and joy to the organism that looks at its wonder? Does the squirrel not become food for another organism to survive its cycle? And did not the spider do its job in controlling and consuming other organisms before its cycle ended?

This sounds a little too clinical to me. Yet it does make some sort of sense. But, I'm still having trouble following his logic.

Me: You make it sound so matter-of-fact, so sterile. What about the emotional turmoil of the people who are left behind because of the loss? It almost sounds like you are justifying usury and killing.

JC: I am not justifying usury or killing and I am not in any way discounting the emotional loss or hurt. I am simply pointing to the fact that there is a cycle. There are reasons for the beginning, the existence and the end of an organism. We are all connected to each other in the same manner that various parts of our bodies are attached to the whole.

Try to think of our cells as many different organisms attached to the whole (the body) and how some of the organisms sustain us more than others. Also note that many of our cells begin, exist and die, this cycle is constant in our bodies, as it is constant in the body of the universe.

I also do not wish to trivialize the events of the cycle, but maybe people should understand that sometimes "dung" happens. Sometimes there are no answers. Sometimes it is just all part of the cycle. This does not make it right or wrong, it just is.

Me: It almost sounds as if we have no control over our destiny.

JC: On the contrary, we do have control, much control. Each time we make a decision, we alter the cycle and not only our cycle, but the ripple effect of our decisions would astound you.

You might want to use the analogy that a domino standing on end represents a decision or choice and when a person makes a decision or choice, he or she automatically strikes the domino and that domino strikes another and another until the person makes another decision or choice.

Me: Ah! The famous Domino Effect!

I feel so comfortable with him that I feel I can now say almost anything and that he will not take it personally.

JC: Yes, smarty-pants, you could say that.

And it seems like he feels the same way about me. This is great! I wish everyone could have this opportunity and feel the way I'm feeling this very moment.

JC: Each decision we make sets a new cycle into motion. A group of connected events bang into each other until another decision or choice is made that will topple another group of dominos in a different direction.

Me: So our control comes with the type and frequency of our decisions.

JC: Yes. Every decision we make causes the Domino Effect, as you called it, and that Domino Effect ripples out in all directions and affects many other organisms at that moment and in the future.

The interesting thing is, although each person may independently make choices, those choices affect others as other people's choices affect you and I. Actually a better example might be drops of water in a pond. Every drop being a person making a choice. As we see more people making decisions, we see more ripples in the pond and even though a person at other end of the pond makes a decision at the same time as you, there is a good possibility that both decisions could eventually ripple into one another. Hence, though we are independent in our choices, we are all interconnected in the fact that our choices do affect others.

Me: I'm afraid you still haven't answered my question as to why bad things happen to good people and why good things happen to bad people.

JC: What you are forgetting is that good things do happen to good people and bad things do in fact happen to bad people.

The problem with many people is they tend to dwell on the bad and need to have answers so they can blame. Yet seldom do people celebrate or look for the root of all of the good that does ripple in their direction.

You see, I truly believe that if more people could make decisions with a mindset that reflected a nonjudgmental, pure, positive co-operative action, the result would be more positive ripples and the negative ripples would be minimized.

Me: I see. So you say I should be concentrating and celebrating all the good stuff and minimize the bad stuff.

JC: You have grasped the concept correctly. No individual's existence in this dimension will be without its ups and downs. The problem is humans constantly aim for a finished product. They look for perfection in an imperfect existence. It must be remembered that this journey is a work in progress and will never be completed. There will always be decisions and choices to make and events to be experienced and learned from.

This concept is going to be difficult for people to grasp.

Me: I think the problem is that many of the experiences that seem to flow in our direction aren't the experiences that we are in fact seeking out. What lesson could I possibly learn from having a friend lose a child to a drunk driver?

JC: Hmm. Offhand, I would say that maybe it was not your lesson to learn. The death of a child affects many people in many different ways and those ways may not be apparent to you today.

Again, I repeat, you question the lesson of the seemingly useless death of a child, but do not question why a person finds money on the street or unexpectedly succeeds at a task thought to be unattainable.

Me: Excuse me? I hope you're not trying to compare the death of a child to getting a windfall.

JC: Not in the least. But consider this, if in fact, we are here to learn and many people use the expression, "we must learn from our mistakes." Then why is it not fair to state, "we must learn from our good fortune," as well?

He got me. His point is well taken. As humans, we do tend to dwell on the negative.

Me: Good point. If we concentrate on the bad and what we learn from misfortune, it would only be logical to try to figure out why we did so well at something.

JC: Can you see how this can help the development of humankind?

Me: I think so. But I'll tell you it's really tough to equate the two incidents you describe as similar in nature.

JC: They are similar only from the standpoint that each is an event, or incident that has occurred and because of each of those events, a decision is made and the ripple effect begins.

All I am trying to point out is that humankind should reflect and learn from all happenings with the underlying aim of finding out what the lesson might be. You should also understand that there might not be a lesson to be learned in every incident. The ripple may have hit you as a ricochet and thus off you to someone else.

Me: *What?* Now you're really screwing with my head.

JC: No, my friend, I am simply reinforcing the fact that we are all interconnected.

Think about how my death and the writing of the scriptures by many others have affected your life. Then some two thousand years later we meet and are having this great interaction. The same ripple effect that killed the child was there for the person who found the money.

So you asked, "Why do bad things happen?" Humankind creates the ripple and those ripples travel in cycles. The problem is that we tend to perpetuate the negative ripples and absorb the positive ones. While the reactions to the negative ripples are heightened, the absorption and inaction to the positive ripples only perpetuates the negative.

We cannot stop the negative ripples that enter our lives, but we can minimize their effect simply by focusing on the positive ripples and learning how they happen. We must learn how to give and receive so many positive ripples that soon the entire world has reversed the ripple effect and good shall encompass all.

Me: A friend of mine asked me this question, "Do you think that everything can be fixed?" How would you answer that question?

JC: That is truly an interesting question, "Can everything be fixed?" First, I would have to add two more questions: "Should everything be fixed?" and, "Is anything really broken?"

I believe there are many who want this journey to be perfect. They believe that if they are perfect, they are Godlike. Keep in mind what I have already stated. Life is a work in progress and as a work in progress it will continue to grow and continue to evolve. People change, relationships change, yet this change has a tendency to frighten people. They want to fix what they "perceive" is broken.

To answer your question and my two questions: "Can everything be fixed?" … of course. "Should everything be fixed?" … no. And, "Is anything really broken?" … not really.

Me: OK. You did it again.

JC: Did what?

Me: You talk in circles. How can everything be fixable and yet not be broken? And how can you say that some things shouldn't be fixed, especially if it's not broken in the first place?

JC: It does sound like I am talking in circles, but you are doing exactly what I believe I was talking about. You are looking for a specific answer, a yes or a no. Life is not like that. Life is fluid. It is constantly changing and it constantly seeks its own level. Sometimes what we think is broken is not really broken and therefore does not need to be fixed, if we change our attitude about something, we have in fact fixed it. And some things are exactly the way they should be and do not need fixing.

Therefore, I say it again. "Can everything be fixed?" Yes, if our Mind God perceives that something is broken or even slightly cracked and we change our thinking, we have in fact fixed the problem.

"Should everything be fixed?" No, because it was not necessarily broken in the first place. We only thought it to be in need of fixing.

And, "Is anything really broken in the first place?" Not really. Remember I am not talking about a cup that has been dropped on the floor and breaks apart. I am talking about our perceptions of the other and our perceptions about life and relationships. Nothing is truly broken it is only evolving. Life is a work in progress. We must learn to embrace this evolution and celebrate the change as humankind moves to the next level.

Me: Tell me, what do you see as the next level?

JC: I see the next level as being the acceptance of the fluidity of life and not being frightened by it. It is time that we come out of our infancy and evolve into full adulthood. That does not mean we have to stop believing in miracles, for they occur around us each day. And we should not stop believing in Santa Claus, for Santa Claus does exist in the minds and hearts of many.

When I say it is time to evolve to full adulthood, we should not give up or abandon our childlike qualities.

Me: How can one be an adult and a child at the same time? That sounds like an oxymoron.

JC: I am not familiar with this term, "oxymoron."

Me: It means that a term contradicts itself. For example, take the term "jumbo shrimp." How can something be "jumbo" and at the same time be a "shrimp"?

JC: Yes, I see.

Me: So when you say that we must evolve into full adulthood yet still be a child, it sounds like an oxymoron.

JC: You misread what I said, for in order to be an adult, you do not have to lose your childlike qualities. Not be a child, but be childlike.

Me: OK. What do you mean by childlike?

JC: Have you ever truly watched children? The way they move, the way they talk and the open and unconditional way they love?

Children are adventurous, they are highly emotional and what I mean by that is that they truly feel. If they are excited or happy about something, you know it. And if they are sad or frightened, you certainly know that as well. They are open communicators and you generally know exactly how they feel. They say what they think. They are spontaneous and they never seem to stop. Children have an amazing energy level and they are highly optimistic.

Me: Then what happens to us as we grow up?

JC: Well, I have already touched on some of this earlier but I do think it is important to really understand how this transition actually occurs. Rather than just teach the children the basics of unconditional love, respect for all life forms and the planet, many parents pass on their own personal phobias, biases and fears. These parents teach their children that whoever is not like them are wrong. They teach them conformity and mediocrity. They even teach their children what is appropriate to discuss. They learn about class difference and that "things" are more important than people. They are taught that their God is the only God and anyone who does not accept *their* God and His ways are wrong and less human. They learn that boys are superior to girls and that success is measured by what you own, not what you do.

My friend, all children are born innocents and they become corrupted by the adult who lost his or her childlike qualities. The adult who believes he or she owns their children as they own chattel are in fact abusing the children. Children are not property to use as labour, to sell or to marry off into a better family. Adults demand respect from children but rarely give respect in return. Does that seem fair?

Me: No. What it does is generate another generation of problems, but how do we raise our children so they know right from wrong? How do we protect them from predators who are out there to do harm to our children? Wasn't it written, "Spare the rod and spoil the child?"

JC: Another bit of writing that is taken too literally. It is important to teach by example. How can one teach tolerance and peace with a weapon in one's hand? How does one teach honesty when one parks in a "no parking" zone? How does one teach acceptance when one tells jokes that hurt people who are different? We must lead by example. "Do unto others as you would have them do unto you." I repeat it and repeat it and repeat it! "Do unto others as you would have them do unto you."

Me: That all sounds so easy, but it can be quite frustrating when you have to keep repeating yourself to a child who doesn't listen.

JC: True. Yet teaching anything takes time and patience, especially with children. Remember they are new to this dimension and are eager to learn, eager to find out why and eager for acceptance.

Try to think of how you would teach a foreigner your language and your customs. How you would take the time to have them understand why you do what you do. And if this foreigner made an error or kept asking why, would you strike them? Would you chastise them? Would you punish them? Or, would you simply continue teaching and explaining until the message was received and understood?

Me: Wow! That's a very good point. We do seem to have more patience with strangers than with our own children.

Tell me, how does one get their point across without becoming angry or violent when the child or the stranger isn't listening?

JC: We must learn how to be assertive but not aggressive. When most people feel that they should be in control and have their wishes obeyed, they can become frustrated. That frustration can bring on anger, hostility and aggression.

Me: I thought that you said you didn't agree with one person having power over another, yet you use the term "obey."

JC: Try to think of most relationships in terms of students and teachers. If we think in these terms, there are going to be times when the teacher will give instruction and the student will obey. Now, I know the word "obey" sounds quite subservient, but in order for the learning to take place in certain circumstances, the student should trust the teacher and carry out the teacher's wishes. This must be coupled with the teacher's primary goal of teaching, not domination or ownership. That is where mutual respect and trust come into play. If one is truly teaching, taking the time to explain the *why* of the situation, then the request will happily and willingly be complied with.

Me: I'm a little confused. There are too many things going on here. How do we lead without becoming power hungry? How do we look for a co-operative action and still not feel we're always giving up or compromising who we are? And how do we protect our children and the weak without becoming aggressive?

JC: Good questions. I can see how they can be a little confusing. Let us keep in mind what I stated earlier. This journey is a work in progress and we are here to learn. That simply means that we are not perfect and we are not infallible. Also, our growth is constant and as we continue to learn, we continue to grow and as we grow, we will trip from time to time. These occasional trips will affect others and, depending on their growth level, their reaction will be somewhere between enlightenment and anger, and their actions will affect even more people, for we are all interconnected.

Let me clarify further by putting this into some sort of order.

First, no one is perfect and everyone makes mistakes.

Second, all that most people want is to be validated, celebrated, and loved.

Third, no one has the right to have power over another. All life must be respected.

Fourth, acceptance is not necessarily agreement.

Fifth, if it is not physically or mentally harming you or those around you, why is it your concern?

Sixth, this journey is simple, do not complicate it.

Seventh, you have the right to be the person you were meant to be as long as you allow all others to be who they were meant to be, keeping in mind that no one knowingly adversely affects the planet or anyone on it.

Before we tackle your three questions, I would ask you what your definition of a leader is.

Me: Well … I think a leader is someone who shows others the way. Someone who teaches, looks after and is responsible for the welfare of those they are leading, for people look up to their leaders.

JC: That is quite true, but I must comment on the terms "responsible for" and "looks after." Could we also add the word "protects"?

Me: Yes, I think that's appropriate.

JC: Herein lies the problem. If as a leader, I think I must protect my followers and be responsible for their welfare, then in fact do I not have to lay down a set of rules in order to control my followers so they will less likely come to harm?

By having this kind of mindset, you can see how leaders are put into positions of power. They become lawgivers who control not to teach, but to minimize damage and keep them in power.

I believe a leader should lead by example. Leadership is earned through respect and deeds that people recognize as an ideal way of being. I do not for one minute believe that a leader is responsible for the actions of those they lead. I do not believe that a leader's goal is to control others and make decisions for them for "their own good."

Me: Can you be more specific?

JC: To me a leader is a teacher and as I said, leads by example. A teacher shows, not forces, the way. A leader is understanding, compassionate and benevolent. People should want to be with a leader, not forced to follow through fear. A leader should only be concerned with enlightenment. A true leader does not seek leadership for his or her gratification. A true leader will always be ready to allow others to lead and a true leader is always willing to learn, share and grow with those around him or her. Finally, leadership is about the empowerment of others.

Me: I understand. That makes a lot of sense.

While we're on the subject of leaders, what causes a Pope to condemn a Queen to death because the Queen is not a Catholic? What would have created the mindset of the Inquisition? How are these people able to do the damage that they do? Is the general public *that* afraid that even when they outnumber their oppressor, they do not stop the injustice?

JC: The problem is: Who shall be the first to make the move? How do we empower people to take this journey into their own hands?

You ask about the leaders and why some are allowed to do what they do. We allow these people to do these things because first, we put them in the position of power and then we allow them to stay there.

Me: I don't know if I can buy that logic entirely, because when I look at history, I see how the Romans conquered others. I see Attila the Hun, Alexander the Great, Hannibal, and in North America, the white men and the natives. Sometimes the evil power of these types just can't be stopped. It seems as though it's man's destiny to take advantage of and rule other men.

JC: Yes, you are right, it does seem that history has shown much evil and destruction. However, along with all of those names that you have mentioned, there have been millions of heroes who have helped eliminate repression and liberated the masses without which we would not be where we are today. Just look at Joan of Arc, King Arthur, Spartacus, Desmond Tutu, Mother Theresa and Nelson Mandela to name a few. I would also mention that not every hero attains national prominence.

You are a hero when you do not step on a spider, but take it outside instead. You are a hero when you pick up a piece of paper from the ground that another person dropped. You are a hero when you hold the door open for another person. You are a hero when you hug someone who needs a hug. You are a hero when you help the homeless. And you are a hero when you smile at a stranger. Anytime you have a positive effect on any other living creature and/ or the planet you are in fact, my friend, a hero of the highest order. It may seem small, but remember "the ripple effect."

False heroism on the other hand is when one seeks recognition for the deeds. These deeds become false, and abusive leaders use their positions to further their own selfish desire and needs. If you do not look for reward for heroism, then the gratitude will come back to you ten fold. A true hero does not look for reward, yet the rewards are many.

Me: So the ideal leader is a teacher, a mentor, a hero, someone who would be interested in expanding the circle, not contracting it.

JC: Yes, that is correct.

Me: Then I have a question about the various religions and sects in the world who seem to be at odds with each other which in turn seems to be perpetrated by the words and actions of the leaders. If most are actually praying to the same God and most use love and respect as the main theme, then why do they fight amongst each other? Why do they condemn and even persecute each other?

JC: A very complicated question. It all comes down to interpretation, leadership and fear. Fear being the primary motivation of all repression. As we talked earlier, difference frightens people but the fear of difference is not quite what I mean in this instance.

This type of fear is about the fear of losing status. It is about the fear of losing power. It is about a little man wanting to be a big man and the fear of rejection. In order to keep adulation this fearful leader must create the enemy without to keep the followers within. The leader uses fear in order to create this enemy in the minds of the people and it is the fear that unifies.

Me: That's sick!

JC: Yes, it is, but these people honestly believe they are right, they honestly believe it is in the best interest for the survival of the unit they are protecting.

Me: You speak as if you are condoning this behaviour.

JC: No, not really. I am only telling you what is fact. The little man with a low sense of self and a need for power over others is the type who uses religion and the law to persecute and create fear in others. Similar to homophobia, the person who yells the loudest about homosexuality is usually the one who has the biggest problem with his or her own sexuality.

Me: That's just like the Shakespearean saying, "the lady doth protest too much, methinks." PROBLEM HERE

JC: Exactly. I like that. I was wondering when you were going to throw in another saying.

Me: Thank you, it just seemed to fit. And I must say that if a fundamentalist leader ever heard you say what you've just said about sexuality, frankly, they'd freak.

JC: Of course they would. Human nature shows us that when we have something to hide, we become more angry or obsessed over a situation. Have you not noticed the difference between a person who has nothing to hide as opposed to a person who is doing something they are not suppose to be doing, when you approach them about the subject in question?

Me: Yes, as a matter of fact, I know several people who actually get pretty angry if you question them about something they forgot to do. I always wonder why they make such a big deal over the situation.

JC: It is quite simple, they understand that they have been caught and they are embarrassed. That embarrassment causes anger. This brings us back to self-concept and the fear of losing.

Me: Losing what?

JC: Losing power, losing position, losing respect and losing friendships. You see, we are constantly told that we must be perfect and are constantly trying to emanate this perfect Godlike persona when in fact no one that I know of could ever reach the heights that some of these so-called righteous leaders demand we attain.

Let us be honest, here. People are fallible, they do make mistakes, they do trip up and they are not perfect. But I must be clear, I am not saying that we are all born sinners and must use this journey to try to be perfect. The pressure is just too great and that is what can cause some of the fear that enters our minds.

No one should be chastised because they made a mistake. I will say it again, this journey is a work in progress and we are only here to learn and share what we learned with others in order for humankind to grow.

Our leaders must learn to mentor, and they must stop the narrow-minded persecution of those who do not agree with them in order to maintain the status quo.

Have you grasped the concept of what makes a good leader?

Me: Yes, I think so. Good leadership isn't about protectionism. It's not about forced servitude. Most of all, a good leader will be a teacher who will allow the student to live the journey to the fullest without trying to mold the student into the model of the teacher.

A good leader will also admit mistakes, admit that he or she doesn't have all the answers, and a good leader won't be afraid to be the student from time to time.

JC: Very good. Now let us see how this helps us answer those three questions that you posed earlier. Do you remember what they were?

Me: I think so … let me see … oh, yes.

How do we lead without becoming power hungry? How do we look for a co-operative action and still not feel we're always giving up or compromising who we are? And how do we protect our children and the weak without becoming aggressive?

JC: Some of these questions we have already partially or even fully answered …

Oh, no, he is going to think that I'm not really listening and that I'm wasting his time.

JC: But maybe I did not explain them to your satisfaction. So, I will go over them again. You must stop me if you need any further clarification.

Hold on, he's not upset. As a matter of fact, he's almost apologizing for not explaining things right in the first place.

Me: I think that you've just shown me by example how to deal with some of these questions. I thought that you'd think I wasn't listening when you have in fact answered the questions. You took it upon yourself to say that maybe you didn't explain them properly in the first place. You didn't blame me for anything. You are taking the responsibility for your actions and not condemning my actions. You're trusting that I want to learn and not being judgmental about my ability to learn. You're allowing me to find my own way without forcing me to blindly accept your explanations.

JC: Excellent! Now see if you can answer the three questions that you posed. I have faith that you will be able to do it.

He reaches forward and gently squeezes my knee as if to say that he's with me and has confidence in my ability to say the right thing. I take a deep breath and I begin ...

Me: First of all, if I'm comfortable with who I am and I'm interested in actually teaching, I don't have to have power over someone else. The power is within me and the greatest power we have is to be able to give up the power. When I give up that power, I don't have to worry about compromise, for there is no need to compromise as I'm looking for co-operative action. Co-operative action eliminates the need for compromise because I'm never feeling that I'm giving anything up for I've already relinquished my need for power. Finally, I can only show others the door. It's up to them as to whether or not they'll choose to enter the door I've pointed to or whether they'll choose their own door. My responsibility ends when I've done the best I can. Each person is responsible for his or her own journey and the leader can only lead those who want to be led. Similarly, a teacher can only teach those who want to be taught.

When I finish, I look into his eyes and see total acceptance and gratification. He taught me well and for now, this time with him is slowly coming to an end.

JC: You have done well, my friend. You truly understand.

Me: But I've so many more questions ...

JC: I know, I know. You have much to digest and should take some time to replay everything we have talked about. Think carefully about how your Mind God creates all. Understand that everyone's personal Mind God is doing the same, creating their own personal reality of their journey. Keep in mind that all of these realities are different and that some of these realities will not be in sync with your own.

You will be a true leader and teacher by accepting the differences in others. You will be a true leader and teacher by not seeking power over other people, but instead empowering people to be who they were meant to be as long as they are not harming others. And finally you will be the ultimate teacher and leader by not judging or allowing yourself to be judged and by being unconditional love as you do unto others as you would have them do unto you.

Knowing all of this, you will fully have understood what I was about and what I was trying to accomplish when I walked this earth some two thousand years ago.

Cupping my cheek with his hands, he looks directly into my eyes with a look of pure unconditional love and commitment. He leans forward and gently kisses my right cheek, then my left. I'm engulfed in pure love energy. I'm shaking, tears fill my eyes and run down my face onto his hands. With both thumbs he softly wipes the tears from my face.

JC: Close your eyes, my friend, for I must go now and my energy light will be blinding.

I hesitate, but do as he asks and close my eyes after drinking in his essence one last time. I can still feel his hands on my face as he continues to talk.

JC: Always remember, through your Mind God, I will be with you and when you need me again, I will return. This journey is yours to live to the fullest and you do have the ability, as does everyone on this planet, to create history. Make that a history that your descendants will be proud to talk about.

I love you, my friend.

Just as I'm about to respond, a bright light permeates through my closed eyes and quickly fills the room. Just as quickly the light leaves. I'm alone on the bed.

I slowly open my eyes and look about the room. To my surprise, the time on the clock still reads 3 am. How could that be? I've learned so much for time to stand still. It must have been a dream. My Mind God must have created the entire event, yet I still feel the strong bond that we have together. I then look down on the bed and there is an indentation in front of me, as if someone had been seated directly across from me. I reach out and feel where he sat. It's warm and I again feel the energy that I had felt earlier.

It's at this moment that I realize, for me this is real and I know that we will have the opportunity to speak again.

I get under the covers and pull them up to my neck. I take one more look around the room, all is quiet and all is peaceful. The ceiling fan is actually relaxing and soothing. I close my eyes and JC's presence is still within me.

Me: I love you, too.

I sink into a deep, peaceful sleep.

Also by Ted Mouradian

BEST in LIFE: *A Guide to Managing Your Relationships with Others, in Your Workplace and, Especially, with Yourself*

This book covers: *Personal Relationships*: Your relationship with yourself. *Relationships with Others*: Family, friends, loved ones, peer pressure, anger management, parent/child. *Corporate Relationships*: Co-workers, employee/employer, interdepartmental, customer relations. *Spiritual Relationship*: Understanding you beliefs, stress management.

Ted Mouradian has over 20 years marketing experience and 15 years as a professional speaker and presenter in Canada, the USA and Australia. He is a confident and humourous motivational speaker.

BEST *in* LIFE
1997 (2nd printing 1999)
Maritimes Arts Projects Productions
ISBN 0-921411-55-3 / US $14.00, CDN $18.69

BEST *in* LIFE is also published in PDF (portable document file) readable on all computers with the free Adobe Acrobat Reader 4.0 software (BJP eBooks, 2000, ISBN 1-896647-17-1, $US 9.00). Purchase it online at the http://PublishingOnline.Com website.

To contact Ted Mouradian about this book or about booking him for seminars, meeting planning and consulting, please call or write:

THE HUMPHRY GROUP
BOX 671
ST CATHARINES ON L2R 6W8
CANADA

Telephone: 905 682-7380, toll-free 1-877-393-3433
Fax: 905 682-1501
E-mail: humphry@iaw.on.ca
www.thehumphrygroup.com

A Selection of Our Titles in Print

A Lad from Brantford (David Adams Richards) essays	0-921411-25-1	11.95
All the Other Phil Thompsons Are Dead (Phil Thompson) poetry	1-896647-05-7	12.95
A View from the Bucket: A Grand Lake and McNabs Island Memoir (Jean Redekopp) memoir, history	0-921411-52-9	14.95
Best in Life: A Guide to Managing Your Relationships ... (Ted Mouradian) self-development, business	0-921411-55-3	18.69
CHSR Poetry Slam (Andrew Titus, ed.) poetry	1-896647-06-5	10.95
Combustible Light (Matt Santateresa) poetry	0-921411-97-9	12.95
Cover Makes a Set (Joe Blades) poetry	0-919957-60-9	8.95
Crossroads Cant (Mary Elizabeth Grace, Mark Seabrook, Shafiq, Ann Shin. Joe Blades, ed.) poetry	0-921411-48-0	13.95
Dark Seasons (Georg Trakl; Robin Skelton, trans.) poetry	0-921411-22-7	10.95
Dividing the Fire (Robert B. Richards) poetry	1-896647-15-4	4.95
Elemental Mind (K.V. Skene) poetry	1-896647-16-2	10.95
for a cappuccino on Bloor (kath macLean) poetry	0-921411-74-X	13.95
Gift of Screws (Robin Hannah) poetry	0-921411-56-1	12.95
Heaven of Small Moments (Allan Cooper) poetry	0-921411-79-0	12.95
Herbarium of Souls (Vladimir Tasic) short fiction	0-921411-72-3	14.95
I Hope It Don't Rain Tonight (Phillip Igloliorti) poetry	0-921411-57-X	11.95
JC & Me (Ted Mouradian) religion	1-896647-35-9	15.99
Like Minds (Shannon Friesen) short fiction	0-921411-81-2	14.95
Manitoba highway map (rob mclennan) poetry	0-921411-89-8	13.95
Memories of Sandy Point, St. George's Bay, Newfoundland (Phyllis Pieroway) memoir, history	0-921411-33-2	14.95
New Power (Christine Lowther) poetry	0-921411-94-4	11.95
Notes on drowning (rob mclennan) poetry	0-921411-75-8	13.95
Open 24 Hours (Anne Burke, D.C. Reid, Brenda Niskala Joe Blades, rob mclennan) poetry	0-921411-64-2	13.95
Railway Station (karl wendt) poetry	0-921411-82-0	11.95
Reader be Thou Also Ready (Robert James) novel	1-896647-26-X	18.69
Rum River (Raymond Fraser) short fiction	0-921411-61-8	16.95
Seeing the World with One Eye (Edward Gates) poetry	0-921411-69-3	12.95
Shadowy:Technicians: New Ottawa Poets (rob mclennan, ed.)	0-921411-71-5	16.95
Song of the Vulgar Starling (Eric Miller) poetry	0-921411-93-6	14.95
Speaking Through Jagged Rock (Connie Fife) poetry	0-921411-99-5	12.95
Tales for an Urban Sky (Alice Major) poetry	1-896647-11-1	13.95
The Longest Winter (Julie Doiron, Ian Roy) photos, fiction	0-921411-95-2	18.69
Túnel de proa verde / Tunnel of the Green Prow (Nela Rio; Hugh Hazelton, translator) poetry	0-921411-80-4	13.95
Unfolding Fern (Robert B. Richards) poetry	0-921411-98-7	3.00
Wharves and Breakwaters of Yarmouth County, Nova Scotia (Sarah Petite) art, travel	1-896647-13-8	17.95
What Morning Illuminates (Suzanne Hancock) poetry	1-896647-18-9	4.95
What Was Always Hers (Uma Parameswaran) fiction	1-896647-12-X	17.95

www.brokenjaw.com hosts our current catalogue, submissions guidelines, maunscript award competitions, booktrade sales representation and distribution information. Broken Jaw Press eBook of selected titles are available from http://www.PublishingOnline.com. Directly from us, all individual orders must be prepaid. All Canadian orders must add 7% GST/HST (Canada Customs and Revenue Agency Number: 12489 7943 RT0001). **BROKEN JAW PRESS, Box 596 Stn A, Fredericton NB E3B 5A6, Canada**